Journey Into Life

A Study on Romans

Woodrow Kroll

Back to the Bible
Lincoln, Nebraska

3,000 printed to date—1995
(1150-231—3M—1095)
ISBN 0-8474-1465-5

The Bible text in this publication is from The New King James Version.
Copyright © 1979, 1980, 1982, Thomas Nelson, Inc. Used by permission.

Printed in the United States of America.

Acknowledgments

Back to the Bible is a diverse ministry. When most people hear the words *Back to the Bible*, they think of a Christian radio broadcast, as well they should. This broadcast is heard daily throughout the world.

But Back to the Bible is much more than radio. The purpose statement of our ministry reads,

> Back to the Bible is a worldwide service ministry whose purpose is to lead believers into spiritual maturity and active service for Christ in the local church and the world and to reach unbelievers with the Gospel of Christ by teaching the Bible through media.

Simply put, Back to the Bible uses every form of media available to us in order to teach the Word and touch the world.

This book, *Journey Into Life*, is the result of a team effort by the Back to the Bible staff, both in the broadcast and print media. Much of the content of this book was aired on the *Back to the Bible* broadcast through my teaching ministry. I spent 11 months teaching Paul's epistle to the Romans to our radio constituency. Now that teaching, in revised form, is available to our reading constituency through this book.

Since *Journey Into Life* is the result of a team effort, I want to acknowledge the outstanding contributions made by members of that team. To Tom Schindler, director of Broadcasting for Back to the Bible; to my cohost on the broadcast, Don Hawkins; to my engineers, Neal Thompson, Kirk Chestnut and Craig Sovereign; and to all the stations throughout the world that aired these messages on the Book of Romans, I acknowledge my sincere gratitude. You have helped lead believers into spiritual maturity and reach unbelievers with the Gospel of Christ.

And to Al Zoller, director of Publications for Back to the Bible; to my assistant and researcher, Allen Bean, who provided help in writing and rewriting what I originally preached on radio; and to my secretary, Cathy Strate, I am indebted. Editorial corrections and suggestions were capably made by Rachel Derowitsch, with assistance from Jill Cornwell. The cover design was guided by the creativity of Kim Johnson.

I willingly express my gratitude to each of my Back to the Bible colleagues who continue to lighten my hands and lengthen my ministry. Thank you.

Contents

Foreword

Life is a journey. Biological life begins with conception, moves through birth and, after commonly passing through childhood, adolescence, adulthood and old age, concludes with death. Only two men in history—Enoch and Elijah—have eluded it. For everyone else, rich or poor, wise or foolish, death is the common denominator.

Spiritually speaking, however, the opposite is true. We begin with death. The psalmist says, "Behold, I was brought forth in iniquity, and in sin my mother conceived me" (Ps. 51:5). That does not mean the act of conception taking place in a marriage relationship is sinful. Rather, the psalmist means that from the moment of conception we are alienated from God. This is the real essence of death. God made humans for fellowship with Him. When our first parents rebelled in the Garden of Eden, that fellowship was lost. We became separated from God. That is why the apostle Paul declares that the wages of sin is death (Rom. 6:23). When we choose to live in sin, we get what we earn—eternal separation from God (i.e., death).

Fortunately, God was not content to leave it that way. While we were dead in trespasses and sins, unable to help ourselves, God the Father sent God the Son, Jesus Christ, to die on our behalf. His agony on the cross, His blood shed for us, settled the debt we could never repay.

When we accept that payment for our sins, God the Holy Spirit comes to dwell within us. Our fellowship with God is reinstated. Those who were dead in sin are made alive. Paul goes so far as to say we are transformed (Gk: *metamorphosed*) into a new creature (2 Cor. 5:17).

But it does not stop there. Like any healthy living creature, we need to grow. When we feed on "the pure milk of the Word" (1 Pet. 2:2), we find ourselves growing from a young, immature Christian into a man or woman of God able to rightly divide the Word of Truth. That is the journey.

As we absorb the Word and practice the Word, we add life unto life (2 Cor. 2:16). Instead of culminating our sojourn in death, we experience death as a turnstile that releases us into a richness of life that we can never fully know here on earth. A Christian's journey is not a journey into death; it is a journey into life.

The apostle Paul traces this journey in the Book of Romans through three major sections, beginning with death (chapters 1–3), birth (chapters 4–11) and growth (chapters 12–16). One of the key verses for the first section is Romans 3:23: "For all have sinned and fall short of the glory of God." The middle section of the letter deals with how we are born—by faith. Romans 5:1 says, "Therefore, having been justified by faith, we have peace with God through our Lord Jesus Christ." Even Jews, with their great religious heritage, need to be justified by that same faith. The third section of Romans addresses how we should live. All living things grow and change. Now that we are reborn into a new relationship with God, we should live our life so as to experience the maximum amount of spiritual growth. Romans 13:13–14 says, "Let us walk properly, as in the day, not in revelry and drunkenness, not in licentiousness and lewdness, not in strife and envy. But put on the Lord Jesus Christ."

No other book in the Bible so completely sets forth the great doctrines of the Christian faith as does Paul's Epistle to the Romans. No other product of the pen has more powerfully confronted the mind of man with the great truths of God. All of man's alibis, all of his pretenses, all of his attempts at self–justification are mightily struck down by the truths of this book. In this letter, Paul's *magnum opus,* every argument that man can muster against the claims of God is demolished with unanswerable logic.

Romans has rightly been called "the Constitution of Christianity," "the Christian Manifesto," "the Cathedral of the Christian Faith." Nowhere is found a more complete compendium of Christian doctrine. In this one letter are the doctrines of justification, sanctification, divine election, condemnation, the perseverance of the saints, total depravity, the last judgment, the fall of man, the revelation of God in nature, the final restoration of the Jews and many others. Romans stands at the head of Paul's epistles as the brazen altar did before the Holy Place in the days of Moses. One could not enter the tabernacle until he passed this altar in the courtyard. Likewise, one cannot enter the great doctrinal portions of the New Testament without first passing Romans. It is the gateway to New Testament truth and the basic training ground for every Christian.

Background

The church at Rome. As the capital of the empire, Rome was the largest and most important city in the first century. Located about 15 miles from the Mediterranean Sea, Rome was a teeming metropolis. In 1941 an inscription was discovered at Ostia indicating that in A.D. 14 the city had a population of 4.1 million.[1]

It is impossible to determine with certainty who founded the Roman church. However, several contenders for this honor can be eliminated. First, it is evident that Paul did not establish this body of believers. Romans 1:10–11, 13 and 15 refer to the fact that Paul had never been to Rome at the writing of this epistle. Second, Peter must be ruled out as well. The view of the present Roman church, which adamantly holds to the Petrine founding of the church in Rome, is based on an erroneous statement of the church historian Eusebius in his *Ecclesiastical History,* Book 11, Chapter 14. He inaccurately records that Peter went to Rome during the second year of the reign of the Roman Emperor Claudius to encounter the impostor Simon Magus, the sorcerer who tried to buy the power of the Holy Spirit (Acts 8:18–19). The second year of the reign of Claudius was A.D. 42. At that time Peter was a pillar in the church of Jerusalem, not Rome (Gal. 2:9). He is frequently mentioned as being active in Jerusalem (Acts 9). He was certainly in Jerusalem through the Council of Jerusalem (Acts 15), which can be dated A.D. 49. Thus, it would have been highly unlikely for Peter to have resided in Rome earlier than that.

Furthermore, Paul greeted by name 26 individuals at the church in Rome. If Peter were bishop of the church by that time, Paul certainly would have mentioned his name as well. Then there is the matter of the beloved physician Luke. In his book *St. Paul the Traveller and the Roman Citizen*, Sir William Ramsay claims that Luke is the most accurate historian of the first century A.D. (pp. 1–10). If Peter, as prominent as he was, had founded

---

[1] Jack Finegan, *Light From the Ancient Past,* (Princeton: Princeton University Press, 1946), p. 288.

the church at Rome, how could Luke have overlooked such an important fact in recording the history of the early church in Acts? In addition, Paul wrote in Romans 15:20, "And so I have made it my aim to preach the gospel, not where Christ was named, lest I should build on another man's foundation." If Peter had founded the church at Rome, why would Paul have been eager to preach there (Rom. 1:15)? These considerations make it appear impossible that Peter established the Roman church.

If neither Paul nor Peter established this church, then who did? Two possibilities exist. The first arises from those present at the Day of Pentecost. Acts 2:9–11 mentions that among those in Jerusalem on that eventful day were "visitors from Rome, both Jews and proselytes." It is quite possible that believing Jews carried their new faith and the message of the Gospel back to the imperial city and founded the church there. Another possibility is that families from Pauline churches in the East settled in Rome and, discovering the faith of each other, gathered to worship independently of the Jewish synagogues. Either way, the church at Rome apparently owed its origin to the migration of Christians from the eastern part of the empire who were converted through their contact with the Gospel there.

It is generally accepted that when Paul wrote Romans there was a church of considerable size at Rome. The contents of this epistle reveal that the Roman church was comprised of both Jews and Gentiles. There was a Jewish community in Rome as early as the second century B.C. It was greatly enlarged by Pompey's conquest of Judea in 63 B.C., when Jewish prisoners of war marched in his grand procession. Cicero refers to the size and influence of the Jewish colony in Rome in 59 B.C. *(Pro Flacco* 66). In A.D. 19 the Jews of Rome were expelled from the city by a decree of Emperor Tiberius. Another mass expulsion took place in the reign of Emperor Claudius (A.D. 41–54). This expulsion caused Aquila and Priscilla to migrate to Corinth, where they encountered Paul (Acts 18:2). But the effects of these upheavals were temporary, for less than three years after the death of Claudius, Paul wrote to the Jewish Christians in Rome and spoke of their faith as a matter of common knowledge.

The original nucleus of the church must have been Jewish. The Gentile element, however, was predominant at the time of Paul's writing. Even though the apostle addressed the Jews in 4:1 when he spoke of Abraham as "our father . . . according to the flesh," there are many direct

10

references to the Gentiles. In his introduction Paul spoke of "obedience to the faith among all nations" (1:5). He desired fruit among the Romans, "just as among the other Gentiles" (1:13). After he reviewed God's dealings with Israel in chapters 9–11, Paul gave concluding admonitions to the Gentiles (11:13). Later, when he wrote to the Philippians from Rome, Paul intimated that it was among the Gentiles that the Gospel had chiefly taken hold in Rome (Phil 1:13; 4:22). A church begun in Jewish hearts had taken on a decidedly Gentile tone.

Place of writing. The contents of the Epistle to the Romans indicate that it was written from Corinth on Paul's third missionary journey. The events of this epistle fit perfectly into the chronology of Acts 20:1–5. Paul's eastern journeys were over; his face was set toward the West (Rom. 15:23–24; Acts 19:21). At this time Paul was headed to Jerusalem with the collection for the poor (Rom. 15:24–27). He did this at the close of his three-month visit to Corinth (Acts 24:17). This collection was emphasized in his epistles to the Corinthians (1 Cor. 16:1–4; 2 Cor. 9:1–5). Romans must have been written a short time after the Corinthian epistles. When he wrote the epistle, Paul mentioned that with him were Timothy, Sosipater, Gaius and Erastus (Rom. 16:21–23). Timothy, Sosipater (Sopater) and Gaius were all mentioned as being with Paul in Corinth during his three-month visit (Acts 20:4). By cross–referencing we note that those mentioned in Romans were the same men who were with Paul at Corinth. This makes it most likely that he wrote the Epistle to the Romans from there.

Date of writing. It is possible to pinpoint the date of writing even further than simply Paul's three–month stay at Corinth. The absence of defensive tactics by Paul and the tranquil tone of the epistle suggest that it was written toward the end of his stay in Corinth, after the troubles there had been quieted. Since all navigation on the Mediterranean ceased between the middle of November and the middle of March, the plans of Phoebe to travel to Rome would hardly have been made before the spring. Thus, it is likely that the date of the Roman epistle was the spring of A.D. 57, although estimations range from A.D. 56 to 58.

Purpose of writing. During the decade A.D. 47–57, Paul spent most of his time intensively evangelizing the territories that border the Aegean Sea and planting churches throughout Asia Minor and Greece. His eastern campaign was now concluded, but his task was by no means complete.

During the winter of A.D. 56–57, which he spent at the house of his Corinthian friend Gaius, he apprehensively looked forward to an immediate journey to Jerusalem. He hoped the gift he bore from the Gentile churches to the poor Jewish saints at Jerusalem would help salve the wounds of controversy and strengthen the bonds between the mother church and the churches of the Gentiles. Once this mission was complete, Paul could continue his dream to labor where no man had labored and build where no man had built. His choice was Spain, the oldest Roman colony in the West. But a journey to Spain would afford opportunity to realize another lifelong ambition—to visit Rome and spend some time with the believers there.

The purpose of his letter to these Roman believers was as follows:

1. To enlist the cooperation and support of the church at Rome for the inauguration of his missionary campaign in the West. Paul realized the strategic and political importance of this city. He needed the assistance of the believers of Rome to launch him into missionary activity in the West as the church at Antioch had done in the East.

2. To obtain the prayer support of the Roman Christians for his forthcoming venture at Jerusalem (15:30–33). Paul was rightly concerned about the outcome of his journey there.

3. To affirm his status as the apostle to the Gentiles. Since Rome was the capital of the Gentile world, it was entirely appropriate that Paul visit the church there.

4. To add validity to their existence by instructing the believers in the faith. Paul knew that the Roman church had come into existence without the authoritative leadership of an apostle of the Lord.

5. To deposit a compendium of theological truth. The capital city of the empire was the natural place for Paul to do so. Because he was apprehensive about the immediate trip to Jerusalem, he perhaps thought the Epistle to the Romans would be his final opportunity to draft a theology of the Christian faith in a written, changeless form. As Adam W. Miller says, "He bequeaths to them in the form of the Epistle the gospel that he would preach to them, should he be permitted to reach there, and if not, they have his letter to read and refer to again and again."[2]

---

[2] Adam W. Miller, *An Introduction to the New Testament,* (Anderson, Indiana: Warner Press, 1972), p. 209.

Paul certainly fulfilled these purposes. This epistle has proven to be one of the bulwarks of evangelical Christianity.

Authorship. The Pauline authorship of the Epistle to the Romans is indisputable and universally acknowledged. On internal grounds, Paul claimed to be the author (1:1). The writer also made personal references that can apply only to Paul (cf. 11:13; 15:15–20). The style, argument and theology are all Pauline as well. On external grounds, quotations from this epistle are found in Clement of Rome, Ignatius, Justin Martyr, Polycarp, Hippolytus, Marcion, the Muratorian Canon and the Old Latin and Syriac Versions. Romans was recognized as Pauline and a canonical writing since the time of Irenaeus, A.D. 130–202.

Although Paul's authorship is indisputable, some critics have questioned the authenticity of chapters 15 and 16. It seems certain that Marcion did not include the last two chapters in his canon. There is also evidence that the early Latin Version ended the epistle with chapter 14 plus the doxology of 16:25–27. However, no extant Greek manuscript omits these chapters.

These two chapters have been assaulted basically on three grounds. Critics charge that (1) the large number of personal greetings in chapter 16 is improbable if Paul had never visited Rome; (2) the commendation of Phoebe was not appropriate to a church Paul had never met; and (3) the suitability of 15:33 as an ending to this epistle makes the addition of chapter 16 unlikely. These criticisms, however, are weak and can be otherwise explained.

The great Roman system of roads would have made it easy for Paul to have met the people mentioned in chapter 16 or to have known them before they moved to Rome. Since Paul was known enough to the church at Rome to have written an epistle to them, he was known enough to have commended Phoebe to them. And although 15:33 does make an appropriate ending, its style is unparalleled in all the Pauline Epistles. The word *grace* occurs in each of Paul's benedictions (cf. Rom. 16:24; 1 Cor. 16:23; 2 Cor. 13:14; Gal. 6:18; Eph. 6:24; Phil. 4:23; Col. 4:18; 1 Thess. 5:28; 2 Thess. 3:18; 1 Tim. 6:21; 2 Tim. 4:22; Titus 3:15; Philem. 1:25), but not in 15:33. Hence, there is no reason not to accept all 16 chapters of the Epistle to the Romans as authentically Pauline.

The importance of Romans. The importance of this epistle cannot be overstated. In the summer of A.D. 386, Aurelius Augustinus, a native of Tagaste in North Africa and professor of rhetoric at Milan, was on the brink of a journey into life. Taking up his scroll he read, "Let us walk properly, as in the day, not in revelry and drunkenness, not in licentiousness and lewdness, not in strife and envy. But put on the Lord Jesus Christ, and make no provision for the flesh, to fulfill its lusts" (Rom. 13:13–14). "No further would I read," he said, "nor had I any need; instantly, at the end of this sentence, a clear light flooded my heart and all the darkness of doubt vanished away."[3] Such was the beginning of Saint Augustine's journey into life.

In November 1515, an Augustinian monk and professor of sacred theology at the University of Wittenberg, Germany, began to expound this epistle to his students. As he prepared his lectures, he became more and more convinced that the just live by faith. "I greatly longed to understand Paul's Epistle to the Romans," he wrote, "and nothing stood in the way but that one expression, 'the righteousness of God.' . . . Night and day I pondered until . . . I grasped the truth that the righteousness of God is that righteousness whereby, through grace and sheer mercy, he justifies us by faith. Thereupon I felt myself to be reborn."[4] Through the reading of this epistle, Martin Luther was born into the family of God, and he began a journey into life.

On the evening of May 24, 1738, John Wesley unwillingly attended a society meeting at Aldersgate Street, where someone was reading Luther's *Preface to the Epistle to the Romans*. Wesley wrote in his journal, "About a quarter before nine, while he was describing the change which God works in the heart through faith in Christ, I felt my heart strangely warmed. I felt I did trust in Christ, Christ alone, for my salvation; and an assurance was given me that he had taken my sins away, even mine; and saved me from the law of sin and death."[5] This event, more than any other, launched the Evangelical Revival of the eighteenth century. Wesley had begun a journey into life.

The great Swiss Reformer John Calvin said of Romans, "When any one understands this Epistle, he has a passage opened to him to the

---

[3] Augustine, *Confessions*, viii. 29.

[4] *Luther's Works*, Weimar edition, Vol. 54, pp. 179ff.

[5] John Wesley, *Works*, 1872, Vol. 1, p. 103.

understanding of the whole Scriptures." Contemporary theologian James I. Packer comments that "there is one book in the New Testament which links up with almost everything that the Bible contains: that is the Epistle to the Romans. . . . From the vantage point given by Romans, the whole landscape of the Bible is open to view, and the broad relation of the parts to the whole becomes plain. The study of Romans is the fittest starting–point for biblical interpretation and theology."[6]

In his *Commentary on Romans*, well–known Greek scholar Frederic Godet observed that "the Reformation was undoubtedly the work of the Epistle to the Romans, as well as of that to the Galatians; and the probability is that every great spiritual revival in the church will be connected as effect and cause with a deeper understanding of this book."[7] What happened to Augustine, Luther, Calvin and Wesley, which left a mark on the world, could happen to us today. So, let the reader beware. Do not begin a serious study of this epistle unless you are willing to bear the consequences. Reading through Romans repeatedly results in revival.

---

[6] James I. Packer, *Fundamentalism and the Word of God,* (Grand Rapids: Eerdmans, 1952), pp. 106ff.

[7] Fredric Godet, *Commentary on Romans,* (Grand Rapids: Kregel Publishers, 1977), p.1.

CHAPTER 1

Getting Ready for the Journey
Romans 1:1–18a

Experienced travelers know that a trouble–free journey begins with making preparations while still at home. Thus, before Paul goes into detail on the journey into life, he wants to prepare his readers for the trip. His writing style is consistent with other authors of the New Testament era. Paul begins the epistle with his name and a salutation. This clarifies who he is and to whom the letter is intended. After a note of thanksgiving for his readers, he launches into a doctrinal section followed by a practical section. Paul wants to make sure his readers are prepared to understand what he is talking about when he uses the term *gospel*. He carefully explains what it means and how it is the foundation for our journey into life.

Who Am I?

Romans 1:1

¹ Paul, a servant of Jesus Christ, called to be an apostle, separated to the gospel of God

One of the icebreakers often played at parties is a game called "Who am I?" The name of a famous person is written on a piece of paper and stuck on your back where you can't see it. The object is to meet other people at the party, ask them for clues and finally figure out the character assigned to you. Many people, however, play this game for real. They truly don't know who they are. As Christians we are "in Christ," but who are we?

The apostle Paul says that he and every other Christian have at least three characteristics that define who we are:

a. *We are first and foremost servants* (v. 1). Paul calls himself **a servant of Jesus Christ**. Literally the word is *slave*.[1] Since a Roman slave was answerable only to his master, Paul knew that he had only one person to please, and that was Jesus. Too often we burn ourselves out trying to please everyone when Christ asks that we please only Him.

b. *We are called people* (v. 1). Paul says he was **called to be an apostle**. He claimed apostleship on at least four grounds: he was a chosen vessel of God (Acts 9:15); he was personally commissioned by Christ (Acts 9:6); he had seen the risen Lord (1 Cor. 9:1–2); and he was the recipient of divine revelation (Gal. 1:10–12, 16–17). Obviously, you and I can't be apostles because we don't meet the above qualifications. Nevertheless, we have a calling. We are "called to be saints" (Rom. 1:7). In the technical sense, we are saints (set–apart ones) the moment we receive Christ as our Savior. On the other hand, since we are saints, we are called to act like saints. This is a life–long process. No Christian can truthfully say he lacks a purpose in life. Our purpose is to be what we already are—saints!

c. *We are separated people* (v. 1). Paul was **separated to the gospel of God.** He was set apart for the ministry of the Gospel long before the Damascus Road experience (Gal 1:15). Even though he would have made an excellent minister to his people, the Jews, in the providence of God, Paul was separated for the work of the Gospel as an apostle to the Gentiles (Acts 9:15). Often we view separation in a negative light: we are separated *from* something. Paul saw it in a positive light, as being sepa-

---

[1] Gk: *doulos*. According to Roman law, a slave had no rights. He could not possess real estate or personal property. He could do nothing without his master's permission. Trench says that this word describes a person who is "in a permanent relation of servitude to another, his will altogether swallowed up in the will of the other" (R. C. Trench, *Synonyms of the New Testament*, p. 29).

rated *to* the Gospel. The focus of the Christian life is not on what we "don't" so much as on what we "do."

The Meaning of *Gospel*

Romans 1:2–4

2 which He promised before through His prophets in the Holy Scriptures,

3 concerning His Son Jesus Christ our Lord, who was born of the seed of David according to the flesh,

4 and declared to be the Son of God with power, according to the Spirit of holiness, by the resurrection from the dead,

In Lewis Carroll's fantasy *Through the Looking Glass*, Humpty Dumpty tells Alice in a scornful voice, "When I use a word, it means just what I choose it to mean—neither more nor less." Unfortunately this happens all too often today. Liberal theologians, cultists (such as Jehovah Witnesses) and others may use the same words as do evangelicals but mean something different by them. Paul begins an interlude starting with verse 2 in order to make sure his readers understand what he means when he says "gospel."[2]

a. *The Gospel is promised* (v. 2). The Gospel is not the product of Paul's mind or anyone else's but was **promised before through His prophets in the Holy Scriptures**. Paul quotes 61 times from the Old Testament, beginning with Genesis 3:15 and ending with Malachi 4:2, to prove the Gospel he preached was not some new invention but something God intended all along. Christians should beware of those who come along with something "new." If it's not a part of God's Word, it's not a part of God's plan.

b. *The Gospel is personal* (v. 3). It centers on a person rather than on a religion, a set of laws or a philosophical discourse. It is **concerning His**

---

[2] Gk: *evangelion*. Originally the word meant "a reward for good tidings"; later, the idea of reward was dropped and it came to stand for the good news itself (W. E. Vine, *Vine's Expository Dictionary of Old and New Testament Words*, p. 167).

19

Son Jesus Christ our Lord, who was born[3] **of the seed of David according to the flesh.** The Gospel is not *about* Jesus Christ; the Gospel *is* Jesus Christ. The Davidic descent of Jesus was the fulfillment of the promise that one from the chosen line would sit on the throne of David forever (2 Sam. 7:13; Jer. 33:17). When we stray from the truth about the Person or work of Christ, we have strayed from the Gospel.

c. *The Gospel is powerful* (v. 4). Christ was **declared**[4] **to be the Son of God with power.** Notice that although Jesus Christ was "born" of the seed of David according to the flesh, He was "declared" the Son of God. Christ was not *born* but eternally *is* the Son of God. This fact was graphically and unmistakably revealed when God raised Him **from the dead.** The resurrection is ample evidence of the power of God. Not even death can stay His mighty hand. That same power is still available today—not the power to control people or amass wealth, but the power to share a Gospel that leads to eternal life. In Acts 1:8 Jesus tells His disciples, "But you shall receive power . . . and you shall be witnesses to Me in Jerusalem, and in all Judea and Samaria, and to the end of the earth."

The Consequence of the Gospel

Romans 1:5–7

5 through whom we have received grace and apostleship for obedience to the faith among all nations for His name,

6 among whom you also are the called of Jesus Christ;

7 To all who are in Rome, beloved of God, called to be saints: Grace to you and peace from God our Father and the Lord Jesus Christ.

---

[3] The usual word for "born" or "begotten" is *genomenou* (Matt. 1:2–16). Paul uses in this verse a related word (*ginomai*), which means "to come into existence." Leon Morris admits this verb "may be used of being born but it is not the usual way of denoting birth" (Leon Morris, *The Epistle to the Romans*, p. 42). Others suggest it means coming from a previous mode of existence (in heaven) to "coming into existence" as a human being.

[4] The word rendered "declared" (*horizō*) has the meaning of "appointed" or "marked out by unmistakable signs." It is used in Acts 10:42 and 17:31 of Christ's appointment as Judge. The resurrection is God's most dramatic sign to an unbelieving world.

Chief Tariri, of the Shapra/Candoshi people in Peru, died August 9, 1994, at the age of 80. Formerly a headhunter, he ended his life as a committed Christian. Taught as a boy to murder men and then shrink their heads to wear as trophies, he spent his last few hours on earth composing songs to the Lord he loved. What made the dramatic difference? He opened his life as a young man to the Gospel of Jesus Christ. He made the journey into life. No one can meaningfully encounter the Gospel message and walk away unchanged. When we receive Christ, we become a new person in Him (2 Cor. 5:17).

What kind of a new person do we become when we trust Jesus Christ and make this journey into life?

a. *We are gifted* (v. 5). Paul declares that **we have received grace and apostleship.** Probably a better translation would be the "grace of apostleship." Paul regards his calling as a heavenly gift. Every person who places his faith in Christ receives at least one gift from the Holy Spirit. Paul mentions at least 20 gifts in three passages (1 Cor. 12:4–9; Rom. 12:6–8; Eph. 4:11–12), but many scholars feel these lists are not meant as a complete catalog. The issue is not "Do I have a gift?" but "What is my gift and how may I use it to build up the body of Christ?"

b. *We are empowered* (v. 5). The purpose of Paul's apostleship is **for obedience to the faith among all nations, for His name.** Paul wanted to bring the nations of the world, both Jew and Gentile, into obedience to the faith (i.e., the body of doctrine that he teaches). But he could not cause this to happen on his own. It took the power of the Holy Spirit working through him to bring men and women to repentance. When God gives a gift, He also supplies the power to use it.

c. *We are claimed* (v. 6). **Among whom you also are the called of Jesus Christ.** The expression "the called" is a favorite one of the apostle to indicate those who have trusted the Lord Jesus as Savior (cf. 8:28). Paul uses the possessive form "of Jesus Christ." Those who surrender their lives to Christ belong to Him. They have been bought with a price and do not belong to themselves. They have been claimed as part of God's family. There are no orphans in His Kingdom.

d. *We are comforted* (v. 7). Paul concludes his salutation by saying, **To all who are in Rome, beloved of God, called to be saints: Grace to you and peace from God our Father and the Lord Jesus Christ.** As God's saints[5] we are the recipients of the comfort of His grace and peace.

21

One of the interesting features of Paul's style is that in every one of his letters these two words appear together. *Grace* and *peace* are never separated (cf. Rom. 1:7; 1 Cor. 1:3; 2 Cor. 1:2; Gal. 1:3; Eph. 1:2; Phil. 1:2; Col. 1:2; 1 Thess. 1:1; 2 Thess. 1:2; 1 Tim. 1:2; 2 Tim. 1:2; Titus 1:4; and Philem. 1:3). One reason for this is that Paul, a Hebrew of the Hebrews but the apostle to the Gentiles, was the bridge between the Jews and Gentiles of the first century church. *Grace* is the typical Greek greeting (*charis*), whereas *peace* is the usual Hebrew greeting (*shalom*). Paul always uses both to bind Jews and Gentiles together in the Lord. It is also true that peace is a by–product of God's grace. It is by grace that we have peace with God (Eph. 2:8). There is a logical progression: grace is first and then comes peace. Without grace there would be no peace.

How to Pray Effectively

Romans 1:8–13

8 First, I thank my God through Jesus Christ for you all, that your faith is spoken of throughout the whole world.

9 For God is my witness, whom I serve with my spirit in the gospel of His Son, that without ceasing I make mention of you always in my prayers,

10 making request if, by some means, now at last I may find a way in the will of God to come to you.

11 For I long to see you, that I may impart to you some spiritual gift, so that you may be established—

12 that is, that I may be encouraged together with you by the mutual faith both of you and me.

13 Now I do not want you to be unaware, brethren, that I often planned to come to you (but was hindered until now), that I might have some fruit among you also, just as among the other Gentiles.

---

5 Sainthood is not to be identified with the practice of canonization, which later arose in the Roman church. The saints (*hagiois*) are those called of God and are "holy" or "set apart" to God. Every Christian is a saint.

Someone once said, "The secret of all failure is prayerlessness." We may blame our circumstances, our finances, even our parents, but more often the real fault lies with our prayer lives. Paul models for us from his own prayer life the ingredients needed for effective prayer.

a. *Effective prayer is thankful* (v. 8). After greeting them, Paul's first words are, **First, I thank my God through Jesus Christ for you all.** The cause for this thankfulness was that their **faith is spoken of throughout the whole world.** So vibrant was the faith of these Roman believers that, like the church of the Thessalonians (1 Thess. 1:6), Paul speaks of it in worldwide terms. The expression "throughout the whole world" is synonymous with *everywhere*. When Paul prayed for these believers at Rome, his first thought was of what they were doing right. They were strong in faith. Certainly they had their weaknesses, but Paul chose to emphasize and be thankful for their strengths. A thankful heart finds it more joyful to pray than to criticize.

b. *Effective prayer is genuine* (v. 9). **For God is my witness, . . .** Paul was not like that hypocrite who loved to pray standing in the synagogues and in the corners of the streets so that he might be seen of men (Matt. 6:5). Paul's prayers were so sincere and genuine that he was not afraid to call even God as his witness. If God were to take the witness stand to testify about your prayer life, what could He say? Could He testify that you remember to pray when you promise people you will? Could He testify that you pray with an attitude of true concern for their needs? Could He testify that you pray regularly? He could if your prayers are genuine.

c. *Effective prayer is constant* (v. 9). This verse continues, **whom I serve with my spirit in the gospel of His Son, that without ceasing I make mention of you always in my prayers.** Paul's prayer life is intertwined with his life of service.[6] He was able to keep these believers in constant prayer because they were part of his service to God. Prayer is not to be treated like cake for special occasions, but like bread for everyday use.

---

[6] The word the apostle uses for service (*latruō*) refers to the function of a priest in the temple and is frequently used by Paul to mean "worship" (cf. Phil. 3:3; 2 Tim. 1:3). A great deal of Paul's priestly service to the Lord was his regular program of intercessory prayer on behalf of other believers (cf. Eph. 1:16; Phil. 1:3; Col. 1:3; 1 Thess. 1:2; 2 Tim. 1:3; Philem. 1:4).

d. *Effective prayer is personal* (v. 9). **I make mention of you** would imply that Paul mentions them by name. In fact, he mentions 26 Roman Christians by name in chapter 16. Paul knew that God was interested in people, not things. His attitude was much like the woman of the house who answered the door and found a census taker. "How many children do you have?" he asked. "Well, let me see," she replied slowly. "There's Agatha, and there's Jonathan and there's . . ." "Never mind the names," the busy man interrupted, "just give me the number!" The woman replied emphatically, "In our family, the children don't have numbers—they have names!" We may paint by numbers, but let us pray by names.

e. *Effective prayer is specific* (v. 10). Paul goes on to say, **making request if, by some means, now at last I may find a way . . . to come to you.** Paul is praying in detail here. He asks the Lord to allow him to visit the church at Rome. Some prayers are so general that you can almost imagine God scratching His head, wondering what is really wanted. Someone once said that nothing becomes dynamic until it becomes specific. In the Old Testament Hannah prayed for a child—but not just any child. She said, "Lord, give me a male child" (1 Sam. 1:11). God answered with Samuel. Joshua prayed for the sun to stand still (Josh. 10:12), and he got it. The key is to be specific.

f. *Effective prayer is submissive* (v. 10). A major concern Paul had was to find a way **in the will of God** to come to the believers in Rome. Sometimes we want something so much that God's will becomes secondary. We're like the young lady who prayed, "Lord, I'm going to marry Joe, so make him a Christian." Prayer would be more dangerous than a loaded pistol if God answered according to our will instead of His. God only promises to answer prayers that match His will.

g. *Effective prayer is purposeful* (v. 11). In the concluding verses of this section, Paul states his purpose in wanting to come to Rome: **For I long to see you** ("I am homesick for you"). This deep longing of Paul to be with the Roman believers rose out of three reasons. First, **that I may impart to you some spiritual gift** (v. 11). Paul wanted to be more than a blessing to them; he wanted to build them up in the faith. Second, Paul desired the Romans to reciprocate, **that I may be encouraged together with you.** Knowing that this local church had not had the apostolic stamp of approval placed on it, Paul wished to visit them to do so. In return, it had been the lifelong desire of the apostle to preach the Gospel in Spain, where no man had laid a foundation. Rome was to be a stopover for that journey. Paul would need lodging, food and Christian fellowship. He desired the Roman believers to provide these for him. Finally, he indicates that his desire was not only to evangelize Spain but also the capital of the Gentile world. He says, **that I might have some fruit among you also even as among other Gentiles.**[7] An evangelist at heart, Paul does not look to Rome simply as a launching pad for further evangelistic effort but as a needy field itself. Prayer is more than words; it reflects the purposes of the heart. If we pray as Paul prayed, we will experience what it means to pray effectively.

The Depth of Debt

Romans 1:14–15

14 I am a debtor both to Greeks and to barbarians, both to wise and to unwise.

15 So, as much as is in me, I am ready to preach the gospel to you who are in Rome also.

The national debt of the United States is so large it is hard to grasp the enormity of it. As U.S. citizens stand on the brink of a debt of four trillion dollars, let us consider what just one trillion dollars could provide: a 40–hour week paycheck at minimum wage for every person in the world; two weeks at Club Med in Bora Bora, French Polynesia, for every person 18 and over in the United States; or an average–size, in–ground, concrete swimming pool for every home owner in the United States. That's mind-boggling!

Yet as astronomical as our national debt is, our spiritual debt to the Gospel is even greater. When we accept God's grace through Jesus Christ, we must say as Paul did, **I am a debtor.** Because of the love of Jesus Christ, which saved us, we are indebted to share the Gospel. Paul makes three observations about this debt:

---

[7] The phrase "other Gentiles" would seem to indicate that although the nucleus of the Roman church was originally Jewish, it is now predominantly a Gentile church.

a. *It is a personal debt* (vv. 14–15). Twice in these verses Paul uses the word *I*. It was not someone else's debt; it was his debt. It is easy to look around in the church and think, *Surely with so many people, someone besides me will do it*. That thinking is reflected in an Eastern story of four brothers. Each was assigned to bring a jar of wine to a feast. Since it was going to be poured together in a common vat, one of the brothers thought he could get away with bringing water instead of wine. *Let the others bear the expense of buying the wine*, he thought. *My failure to contribute will never be noticed*. When the wine was poured out at the feast, however, it was all water. Each of the brothers had thought alike.

Unless it gets personal, it probably won't get done. Instead of letting "George do it," we need to take to heart a note that appeared in a church bulletin: "George doesn't attend here anymore."

The personal nature of this debt is reflected in Isaac Watts's hymn *At the Cross*: "But drops of grief can ne'er repay the debt of love I owe. Here, Lord, I give myself away 'tis all that I can do."

b. *It is a worldwide debt* (v. 14). Paul says he is indebted to share the Gospel with **Greeks and to barbarians, both to wise and to unwise**. From the golden age of Athens under Pericles in the fifth century B.C. until the decline of the Grecian empire, Greece was more highly civilized and educated than any other society of its time. The Greeks (and those who assimilated their culture, such as the Romans[8]) considered themselves the elite. In the Greek mind there were only the Greeks and the barbarians[9] (everyone else). In God's mind, however, there are only the saved and the unsaved (1 John 5:12). No matter how cultured or educated a person might be, he is still lost without Jesus Christ. Culture is no substitute for salvation.

The same is true for the **barbarian**. Ignorance is no excuse. As Paul later points out, God has revealed Himself in nature, so everyone is accountable for his attitude toward Him.

---

[8] The Roman orator–author Cicero (106–43 B.C.) places Greece and Rome in the same category in his treatise *De Finis, On Ends*. He says, "not only Greece and Italy, but also every foreign country." Therefore, Paul can readily say to the Romans that he is debtor both to the Greeks (Gk: *Hellenes*), including the Romans, and the less civilized barbarians (*barbaroi*).

[9] Barclay notes that a barbarian was literally "a man who says bar–bar, that is to say a man who speaks an ugly and an unharmonious tongue in contrast with the man who speaks the beautiful, flexible language of the Greeks" (William Barclay, *The Letter to the Romans*, pp. 17–18).

c. *It is an immediate debt.* Paul says **I am ready**—not tomorrow, not next week, but right now. Paul tells Timothy, "Be ready in season and out of season. Convince, rebuke, exhort, with all longsuffering and teaching" (2 Tim. 4:2). Failing to be ready can result in tragedy for multitudes. During the Arab–Israeli war of 1967, an American reporter was flying over the Sinai desert with an Israeli soldier. Suddenly, he spotted a group of some 50,000 stranded Egyptian soldiers. It was obvious that they were dying of thirst. The situation was reported immediately, but by the time a plan was readied to bring relief, thousands of the soldiers had perished. When we are not ready to share the Gospel, thousands will lose more than their lives; they will lose their souls.

Paul was not only able and willing, but he was ready to preach. He was a clean vessel, not just a chosen vessel. He was ready to be used of God. Paul was like the old country preacher who, when asked how he prepared his Sunday sermon, said, "I read myself full, think myself clear, pray myself hot and let myself go." Many believers are not ready to be let go because they are not "read full," nor clear–minded about Christian doctrine, nor "hot" (i.e., fervent) in prayer. How ready are you right now to be used of God?

All Hail the Power

Romans 1:16–18a

16 For I am not ashamed of the gospel of Christ, for it is the power of God to salvation for everyone who believes, for the Jew first and also for the Greek.

17 For in it the righteousness of God is revealed from faith to faith; as it is written, "The just shall live by faith."

18a For the wrath of God is revealed from heaven against all ungodliness and unrighteousness of men,

On November 9, 1965, an automatic control device that regulates the flow of electrical current failed in Queenston, Ontario. This caused a circuit breaker to remain open, resulting in a surge of excess current that was transmitted throughout the northeastern United States. Generator safety switches from Rochester, New York, to Boston, Massachusetts, were automatically tripped to protect them from damage. Power generated by plants south of this area rushed in to fill the vacuum. These plants quickly became overloaded and automatically shut themselves off as well. The consequent power failure eventually encompassed an area of more than 80,000 square miles and included such major cities as Boston, Buffalo, Rochester and New York.

Such a failure was a great embarrassment to the power companies (not to mention an inconvenience for their customers), but Paul says we never have to worry about that with the power of God. He says, **For I am not ashamed**[10] **of the gospel of Christ, for it is the power of God**. Paul then shares three areas where that power is revealed:

a. *God's power is revealed in salvation* (v. 16). He says, **for it is the power of God to salvation for everyone who believes**. The Gospel, through the agency of the Holy Spirit of God, does what no human reasoning or argumentation can accomplish—it compels men to face the reality of their own sin and guilt, the inevitability of divine judgment and the need for a perfect substitute to make atonement for sin, if man is to survive at all. The Gospel is the explosive power[11] that blasts away self–complacency, self–delusion and sinful self–reliance. It is the power that sets us off on a journey into life and assures a safe arrival at our journey's end in heaven. Nothing else can do it.

b. *God's power is revealed in righteousness* (v. 17). Paul says, **For in it** (the power of the Gospel) **the righteousness of God is revealed**. Righteously is the way God treats us. Before the foundation of the world, God purposed to reveal His righteousness (Eph. 1:4). After the Fall He

---

10 Paul may have had our Lord's warning in the back of his mind (Luke 9:26). Someone might well ask why Paul could have been ashamed of the Gospel. Perhaps he would be ashamed to spread the Gospel because of the fierce persecution against those who had come to believe in this message. As a Jew, Paul could have been ashamed of the Gospel because the Jews abhorred it as subverting the Law. As an educated man, he might have been ashamed because to the wise Greek, the Gospel was sheer foolishness. He may have been ashamed of the Gospel of Christ because the pagans branded Christians as atheists, a stigma no Pharisee could tolerate. This atheism was not a theoretical denial of the existence of the gods (Gk: *asebeia*), but a practical refusal to recognize pagan deities as truly God (*atheos*). For those whom the Romans considered to be "Christian atheists," the consequences were severe, such as forced labor in mines or even capital punishment.

11 Power can come from either ability or authority. The British writer G. K. Chesterton distinguished it this way to a luncheon guest: "If a rhinoceros were to come charging into this restaurant, I would admit he had great power. But I would also be the first to rise and assure him that he had no authority whatever." The word used here (Gk: *dynamis*) emphasizes one's ability. God has the ability (the strength or power) to save.

promised to reveal His righteousness (Gen. 3:15), but it was not until Christ came that His righteousness became tangible. Through Christ's death on the cross we can now see God's righteousness. We are unrighteous, unholy and unlovely. Yet Christ died for us (1 Thess. 5:9–10).

Furthermore, by faith we can personally experience God's righteousness. In fact, Paul quotes the prophet Habakkuk, who says, **The just** (righteous) **shall live by faith** (Hab. 2:4). This faith implies more than mere acceptance of Christ's righteousness for salvation. It implies a lifestyle that is characterized by faith and righteous living. It was this truth that excited Martin Luther and initiated the Protestant Reformation. When a person discovers that righteousness is not in a church, a religion or in doing penance but is in a person, Jesus Christ, it changes his life.

c. *God's power is revealed in wrath*[12] (v. 18). People want to believe only that "God is love." This is true, of course, but real love will be wrathful toward that which harms the object of that love. God's wrath is toward **all ungodliness and unrighteousness** because these are the things that destroy those He died to save.

Sometimes it seems like evil always prevails. Wicked men are frequently in positions of power and authority. They often control great wealth and large armies. The assurance we have, however, is that God is far more powerful than they. In speaking of the wicked the psalmist says,

Surely You set them in slippery places;
you cast them down to destruction.
Oh, how they are brought to desolation, as in a moment!
They are utterly consumed with terrors (Ps. 73:18–19).

God will never rest until all evil is exterminated.

---

[12] The word *wrath* (Gk: *orgē*) appears 36 times in the New Testament. Paul uses the word 21 times; 12 times in Romans alone. Wrath is God's personal (although never malicious) reaction toward sin. God could not be free from wrath unless He were also free from all concern about His moral universe.

CHAPTER 2

Point of Departure
Romans 1:18b–2:29

International airports are fascinating places. They are like a microcosm of the larger world. They are a point of departure for a multitude of people. Some of these people are short, others tall. Some are Oriental, others Occidental. What's more, these people come from very different places. Some have flown out of O'Hare in Chicago; others out of Kennedy in New York; still others began their journey overseas. At this moment, however, they are bound together by a common point of departure.

The same is true spiritually. Having completed the salutation of his letter to the Romans, Paul is now ready to discuss our common point of departure. The world is filled with a variety of people. Some are heathen—those who make no pretense at spirituality. Their motto is, "If it feels good, do it!" Others are people of high moral values (moralists), but they have no spiritual concerns. Still others are very religious. They have all kinds of rules for living the "spiritual life." Yet Paul claims each group has a common point of departure—they need a Savior.

Beginning in verse 18, Paul lays the groundwork for his case against man's self–righteousness. His aim is to show that the whole world is morally bankrupt, unable to receive a favorable verdict at the Judgment Seat of God and desperately in need of divine mercy and pardon.

The Heathen

Romans 1:18b—23

18b who suppress the truth in unrighteousness,

19 because what may be known of God is manifest in them, for God has shown it to them.

20 **For since the creation of the world His invisible attributes are clearly seen, being understood by the things that are made, even His eternal power and Godhead, so that they are without excuse,**

21 **because, although they knew God, they did not glorify Him as God, nor were thankful, but became futile in their thoughts, and their foolish hearts were darkened.**

22 **Professing to be wise, they became fools,**

23 **and changed the glory of the incorruptible God into an image made like corruptible man—and birds and four-footed beasts and creeping things.**

We sometimes speak of the "innocence of childhood." Yet anyone who has seen a two-year-old throw a tantrum knows that this is just a figure of speech. In the same way, some people speak of the "innocent heathen" as though somewhere there abides this pristine group of people who know nothing of sin. This always raises the question, "How could God allow such individuals to go to hell?"

Yet the truth is that such a group is purely a figment of the imagination. Paul says that instead of being innocent, these people are guilty of suppressing[1] the truth in unrighteousness.[2] How do we know this is true? Because:

a. *God reveals His truth in our conscience* (v. 19). Every group of people has a list of rights and wrongs. The categories may differ somewhat from culture to culture, but the underpinning is the same. For example, in some cultures it is wrong to kill anyone at any time. In other cultures it is wrong to kill someone from your tribe, but you can kill

---

[1] The word *suppress* (Gk: *katechō*) carries the meaning of "hold down," "to restrain" or "keep back." The meaning of this word is clearly seen in the way it is used in Luke 4:42: "Now when it was day, He [Christ] departed and went into a desert place. And the crowd sought Him and came to Him, and tried to keep Him from leaving them." Paul contends that the heathen restrained or held back the truth of God's righteousness. They refused to recognize it themselves and sought to keep others from knowing about it as well.

[2] Unrighteousness has to do with morality, our relationship to our fellowman. Ungodliness has to do with religion, our relationship to a sovereign God. Unrighteousness is sin against the will of God. Ungodliness is sin against the being of God. Man is both a moral sinner (he is unrighteous) and a religious sinner (he is ungodly).

someone from outside your tribe. Yet to one degree or another, killing is viewed as wrong. Where did such an idea come from? God put it in their conscience. Paul says, **because what may be known of God is manifest in them.** There is an inner sense of what is right and wrong even though it has become warped through the Fall.

b. *God also reveals His truth in nature* (v. 20). God didn't stop with just one source of revelation; He also revealed Himself in nature. J. B. Phillips translates verse 20 as, "For since the beginning of the world the invisible attributes of God, for example, his eternal power and divinity, have been plainly discernible through things which he has made and which are commonly seen and known, thus leaving these men without a rag of excuse." Anyone can look at the orderliness of the universe, the creative variety within nature, the complexity of matter that makes up life and recognize there is an intelligent being guiding it. **His invisible attributes are clearly seen** by those willing to use their eyes. Man's mind is capable of drawing obvious conclusions from effect to cause. Sir Isaac Newton had a model of the solar system made. An unbelieving friend stopped by and admired the miniature cosmos. "Who made it for you?" he asked. "Nobody," Newton replied. "What do you mean, 'nobody?' his friend responded. "That's right," Newton continued. "All those cogs and belts and gears just happened to come together." The friend got the message. An orderly creation demands an orderly Creator.

To animals, the phenomena of nature may just be a spectacle before their eyes that makes no impression on their minds. But to man, nature should awake wonder, awe and a basic idea of God and His righteousness—**even his eternal power and Godhead.** Nature does not merely give the impression that God is an abstract principle but a real person, the Supreme Person, transcendent above His creation and not part of it. The testimony of nature alone is sufficient to lead men to an understanding of the personal, righteous nature of God, **so that they are without excuse.**

c. *But God goes even further to reveal His truth by placing it in our hearts* (vv. 21–23). While our conscience deals with right and wrong, our heart deals with innate needs. Man has a need to worship something. Long before people wrote theology books (or were even able to write), they buried their dead with evidence that they believed in some kind of an afterlife. There is no group of people today that does not have at least a rudimentary religion. The people Paul speaks of also felt a need to worship, but they **changed the glory of the incorruptible God into an image made like corruptible man—and birds and four-footed beasts and creeping things.** They chose to worship the created rather than the Creator. They became idolaters. Consequently, they also became fools. Only a fool would choose to neglect the greater in favor of the lesser.

When God Quits

Romans 1:24–32

24 Therefore God also gave them up to uncleanness, in the lusts of their hearts, to dishonor their bodies among themselves,

25 who exchanged the truth of God for the lie, and worshiped and served the creature rather than the Creator, who is blessed forever. Amen.

26 For this reason God gave them up to vile passions. For even their women exchanged the natural use for what is against nature.

27 Likewise also the men, leaving the natural use of the woman, burned in their lust for one another, men with men committing what is shameful, and receiving in themselves the penalty of their error which was due.

28 And even as they did not like to retain God in their knowledge, God gave them over to a debased mind, to do those things which are not fitting;

29 being filled with all unrighteousness, sexual immorality, wickedness, covetousness, maliciousness; full of envy, murder, strife, deceit, evil-mindedness; they are whisperers,

30 backbiters, haters of God, violent, proud, boasters, inventors of evil things, disobedient to parents,

31 undiscerning, untrustworthy, unloving, unforgiving, unmerciful;

32 who, knowing the righteous judgment of God, that

those who practice such things are worthy of death, not only do the same but also approve of those who practice them.

Everybody has days when what they want most is simply to be left alone. They don't want to answer the door, pick up the phone or even turn on the TV. They want to be inaccessible, at least for a while. This may be OK when we are dealing with our coworkers or friends, but it is a terrible disaster when it applies to God. There comes a time when God finally says, "All right, have it your way. I'll leave you alone if that is what you want." Paul then outlines a series of consequences for those who turn their back on God:

a. *They become enslaved to idolatry* (v. 25). They both **worshiped and served the creature rather than the Creator.** What begins in worship ends in servitude and the "creature" is a cruel taskmaster. A missionary tells of watching a woman in India toss her young child into crocodile-infested waters as an offering to her god. Tears rolled down her cheek, but it was a necessary sacrifice to appease the one she served. The gods of our own making have no pity or mercy.

b. *They become enslaved to immorality* (vv. 24, 26–27). The next step down from idolatry is immorality. **God also gave them up[3] to uncleanness.[4]** In the ancient world idol worship was often associated with sexual immorality. In Corinth, where Paul likely wrote the Book of Romans, stood the temple of Aphrodite (or Artemis), the goddess of love. One thousand sacred prostitutes "ministered" at this temple to the wanton desires of the worshipers—thus the Greek proverb, "It is not every man who can afford a journey to Corinth." **For this cause God gave them up to vile passions.** These "vile passions" were passions of infamy. The apostle goes on to explain that **their women exchanged the natural use for what is against nature.** Sexual perversion frequently accompanies idolatry. **Likewise also the men . . . burned in their lust for one another; men with men.** Homosexuality is likewise the outgrowth of idolatry. Although today the

---

[3] God is not being vindictive. Throughout the Bible, when God gives up, it is an act of mercy. In letting people experience the consequences of their behavior, He hopes they will realize the futility and emptiness of their desires and return to Him.

[4] As seen by Paul's usage of this term elsewhere (cf. 2 Cor. 12:21; Gal. 5:19; Eph. 5:3; Col. 3:5; 1 Thess. 4:7), *uncleanness* means sexual aberration (literally, "passions of dishonor") by which people would **dishonor their own bodies between themselves.**

world seeks to popularize and legitimize homosexuality, it is nevertheless despicable to God and condemned by Him. God never overlooks this blatant misuse of the body; therefore, those who have engaged in this perversion receive **in themselves the penalty of their error which was due.**

c. *They become enslaved to foolishness* (v. 28). **God gave them over to a debased mind.** The word *debased* means "undiscerning." Since they had suppressed the truth God revealed to them, the only thing left was the foolishness of the world. Someone once said that the man who stands for nothing falls for everything.

Foolishness is rampant in society. For example, real estate ads in major newspapers can no longer describe their property as having an "ocean view" (this might offend the blind) or being within "walking distance" of a destination (an affront to the wheelchair–bound). They also cannot use the expression "master bedroom" (indicates a sexist attitude) or "executive" (could be racist; most executives are white).[5]

The heathen did not retain God in their knowledge and, consequently, for the third time in almost as many verses, the apostle records that God gave them up (or over) to what they wanted all along. When He did so, the results were disastrous. Thinking themselves to be wise, they became fools.

d. *They become enslaved to rebelliousness* (vv. 29–32). **Being filled** expresses (by the Greek perfect tense) that the heathen were not simply tainted by the catalog of sins that follow, but were in fact saturated with them. Thus the ugly character traits listed as the result of abandonment by God include **unrighteousness** (or injustice[6]); **wickedness,[7] covetousness[8]**

---

[5] John Leo, "On Society," *U.S. News & World Report*, December 5, 1994, p. 26.

[6] Gk: *adika* is the opposite of justice, which meant to the Greeks "giving to God and to men their due." Thus, an unrighteous man robs both man and God of their rights. He does not care about their needs or concerns. When a man makes himself the center of his existence, he excludes both God and his fellowman.

[7] Gk: *poneria* is defined by the Greeks as "the desire to do harm." Barclay says, "It is the active, deliberate will to corrupt and to inflict harm" (Barclay, *The Letter to the Romans*, p. 34). It is used to describe Satan (the evil one) in Matthew 6:13.

[8] Gk: *pleonexia* is an aggressive vice. It will take that which it has no right to take; it will violate honor and honesty; it will trample on the hearts and bodies of any who stand in the way of its ambitions. It is a devouring greed that knows no law or limits.

(grasping for more than is needed), **maliciousness**[9] . . . . **whisperers, backbiters, haters of God, violent, proud, boasters, inventors of evil things,**[10] **disobedient to parents, undiscerning, untrustworthy, unloving, unforgiving, unmerciful.** This gallery of iniquity was not only true of the first century heathen world but reads much like our newspapers today.

These things were not done in ignorance: **who, knowing the righteous judgment of God, that those who practice such things are worthy of death.** Heathens are aware of God's displeasure with these activities. They fully realize the consequences of their sin, yet they continue to defy the Lord God of heaven. Not only that, but they **approve of those who practice them**. They act as cheerleaders, encouraging others to rebel against God.

Are the heathen lost? Yes, the entire heathen world is lost, desiring evil, desperately wicked and deserving condemnation.

The Moralist

In the last section (Rom. 1:18–32) Paul painted a picture of the deplorable condition of the heathen. He now turns to a group of people who would vigorously deny they had anything in common with immoral libertines. Instead, they prided themselves on their strong code of ethics while loudly and publicly condemning the activities that the heathen revel in. But Paul contends they have no basis for their judgmental attitudes.

Some people have misused this passage to avoid accountability for their sins. "Judge not lest you be judged" is their cry. Yet Paul does not mean that it is always wrong to judge. Judgment is legitimate if (1) it is a matter of discernment rather than condemnation. In fact, God's people are responsible to distinguish between truth and error based on the clear teaching of Scripture. (2) It is a matter of judging fruit rather than motives. Only God can see the heart. (3) It is a matter of first judging ourselves. We need to take the log out of our own eye before we remove

---

[9] Gk: *kakia* is an evil habit of mind. It is the seedbed for all other vices.

[10] Gk: *epheuretas kakōn* describes someone who is so jaded that he has to come up with new forms of sin to reach the same level of excitement.

the speck from our brother's (Matt. 7:4). But even if judging isn't always wrong, it is something we never want to take lightly.

When Being Good Isn't Enough

Romans 2:1-8

1 **Therefore you are inexcusable, O man, whoever you are who judge, for in whatever you judge another you condemn yourself; for you who judge practice the same things.**

2 **But we know that the judgment of God is according to truth against those who practice such things.**

3 **And do you think this, O man, you who judge those practicing such things, and doing the same, that you will escape the judgment of God?**

4 **Or do you despise the riches of His goodness, forbearance, and longsuffering, not knowing that the goodness of God leads you to repentance?**

5 **But in accordance with your hardness and your impenitent heart you are treasuring up for yourself wrath in the day of wrath and revelation of the righteous judgment of God,**

6 **who "will render to each one according to his deeds":**

7 **eternal life to those who by patient continuance in doing good seek for glory, honor, and immortality;**

8 **but to those who are self-seeking and do not obey the truth, but obey unrighteousness—indignation and wrath,**

When a little girl was told that the sun was 95 million miles away, she asked, "Did you measure from the top of my house or the bottom?" Obviously, it would make no difference. A few feet one way or the other would not matter. The same is true when we compare our righteousness to God's. Some people do live a better life than others. Yet when compared with the perfection of God, none of us have any room to brag.

The apostle knew that the self-righteous moralists would say a hearty "amen" to his assessment of the heathen. So Paul expands his argument to show that "all ungodliness and unrighteousness of men" includes the moralists as well as the debauched heathen. The most moral of men are condemned on three counts:

a. *They are condemned by their own judgments* (v. 1). **For in whatever you judge another you condemn yourself; for you who judge practice the same things.** It is obvious that the moral man was not involved in the sexual deviations of the heathen, or else Paul could not call him moral. But he was inwardly living in an identical manner as the heathen was living outwardly. Perhaps the moral man did not commit adultery, but did he lust? Our Lord put them in the same category in Matthew 5:27-28. Maybe the moral man did not steal, but did he covet? Stealing and covetousness are listed together in Mark 7:22. Maybe the moral man did not commit murder, but did he hate? The Bible says if you hate your brother you are guilty of murder (1 John 3:15). The behavior that the moralist condemns as wrong in others is present within himself— it just isn't as obvious. Therefore, when the moral man condemns them, he also condemns himself.

b. *They are condemned by the truth* (vv. 2-5). When God judges it is always according to the truth. He never changes the facts. **But we know that the judgment of God is according to truth against those who practice such things.** The moralist may attempt to hide the facts, but God always exposes them. His searching eye always ferrets out the truth.

A drug runner was trying to smuggle a shipment of illegal drugs hidden in bales of cotton past the Coast Guard. In spite of his devious efforts, he was spotted by a patrol boat, which took up pursuit. The smuggler was determined not to be caught with the contraband, so he began to throw the cotton bales overboard. What he didn't notice, however, was that the bales didn't sink. Instead of hiding his crime, he created a chain of evidence that led the authorities directly to him.

The effort to hide the truth from God is equally futile. To deny what God knows to be true is to **despise the riches of his goodness**[11] **and**

---

[11] *Goodness* (Gk: *khrēstotēs*) means more than "being good" or "doing the right thing." It also carries the thought of being kind. In John 8:1–11 (the story of the woman taken in the act of adultery), the Pharisees were "right" while Jesus was "good."

forbearance[12] **and longsuffering.**[13] It is better to confess than to deny. In fact, Scripture says that is the only way to deal with our sins (1 John 1:9). The difficulty the moralist encounters is that his pride will not allow him to acknowledge he needs the goodness of God as much as the heathen does. Paul notes, **But in accordance with your hardness and your impenitent heart you are treasuring up for yourself wrath in the day of wrath and revelation of the righteous judgment of God.** After years of glossing over his personal sin and guilt, the moral man will find on the day of God's righteous judgment that he has as much to account for as the heathen.

c. *They are condemned by their deeds* (v. 6). Everyone wants to blame someone or something else. A woman drowned her two children and blamed it on the abuse she experienced as a child. Another individual embezzled more than $2 million and claimed it was the result of stress in the workplace. But Scripture says that God **will render to every man according to his deeds**.

When unsaved men receive their final sentence at the Great White Throne Judgment (Rev. 20:11–15), salvation will not be the issue. This is a judgment to determine the degree of punishment according to their deeds. By the same token, at the Judgment Seat of Christ, where only believers appear, God will reward Christians according to their deeds. In both situations, however, when the journey is over, God will expect everyone to take responsibility for his behavior. It is our deeds, not our excuses, that will count with God.

Appointment With Destiny

Romans 2:8–16

8 but to those who are self-seeking and do not obey the truth, but obey unrighteousness—indignation and wrath,

9 tribulation and anguish, on every soul of man who does

---

[12] The word used for forbearance (Gk: *anochē*) means to declare a truce. But it is a truce with a purpose—to allow sinners time to repent and turn from their sins.

[13] Longsuffering (Gk: *makrothymia*) describes patience as it is exercised toward people. It is used to characterize a man who has the power to extract vengeance but does not.

evil, of the Jew first and also of the Greek;

10 but glory, honor, and peace to everyone who works what is good, to the Jew first and also to the Greek.

11 For there is no partiality with God.

12 For as many as have sinned without law will also perish without law, and as many as have sinned in the law will be judged by the law

13 (for not the hearers of the law are just in the sight of God, but the doers of the law will be justified;

14 for when Gentiles, who do not have the law, by nature do the things in the law, these, although not having the law, are a law to themselves,

15 who show the work of the law written in their hearts, their conscience also bearing witness, and between themselves their thoughts accusing or else excusing them)

16 in the day when God will judge the secrets of men by Jesus Christ, according to my gospel.

An old saying assures us that "nothing is certain but death and taxes." If that were true, we would have to add one more certainty— judgment. Paul says in verse 16 that **God will judge**. No question exists in Paul's mind. The moralist will face judgment just as certainly as the heathen. Paul describes that judgment in verses 8–16.

a. *God's judgment will be terrible* (vv. 8–9). Cable TV mogul Ted Turner told a group of people at a Baptist church luncheon, "I'm looking forward to dying and going to hell because that's where I'm headed." If he only knew the truth about his destination, he would not be so eager. Some people have the idea that hell is a place where they can spend eternity partying with their friends. On the contrary, Paul says, it is a place of **indignation and wrath,**[14] **tribulation**[15] **and anguish.**[16] Hell should never

---

[14] Gk: *orgē* (indignation) and *thymos* (wrath) are often found together (Eph. 4:31; Col. 3:8; Rev. 19:15). Although sometimes used interchangably, *thymos* carries the thought of a boiling agitation, while *orgē* a more abiding and settled habit of mind (Trench, *Synonyms of the New Testament*, pp. 123–124).

[15] Gk: *thlipsis* literally means to "press" or "squash." It is used of trampling on grapes to squeeze the juice out. It implies severe discomfort and suffering.

[16] Gk: *stenochōria* means dire calamity or extreme affliction.

be taken lightly. Billy Sunday used to say, "I'd sooner be a foot out of hell and headed for heaven than a foot out of heaven and headed for hell."

b. *God's judgment will be impartial* (v. 11). **For there is no partiality**[17] **with God.** It was a common expectation in the court system of Paul's day that a judge would side with the rich and important rather than the poor and insignificant. Perhaps that is why the Bible is full of exhortations to those who judge to do so fairly. It is human nature to be biased toward one side or the other. Fortunately, that is not God's nature. The ground around God's judgment seat is absolutely level.

c. *God's judgment will be complete* (v. 16). Paul describes it as **the day when God will judge the secrets of men**. Socrates once made the statement that he was the wisest of the Athenians. Hearing that from such a humble man, people were shocked. "How can you say that?" they asked. Socrates replied, "Well, there are a great many of the Athenians who think they know, and I know I do not know; therefore I am the wisest of the Athenians." If we are totally honest, we would have to say along with Socrates, "I know I do not know." When we try to judge, we are prone to error because we often do not know all the facts. But God knows it all, including the deepest, darkest secrets of our hearts. Not even those things will escape His judgment.

The Religious

When you study the life of Christ, you find that His most hostile enemies were not the sinners but the religious. It was the Jewish religious leaders who made sure that Jesus was tried, convicted and crucified. The same was true for the apostle Paul. He was hounded from city to city by a group of men called Judaizers—those who claimed to be Christians yet who felt that Gentile converts should be circumcised and keep at least part of the Jewish law in order to be saved. They vigorously opposed Paul's teaching of salvation by grace alone. Invariably, religious people put more faith in their religion than in their Lord.

---

[17] The Authorized Version translates this, "For there is no respect of persons with God." God does not respect one person over another. Literally, the Greek word (*prosopō-lempsia*) means to "receive face." It does not appear before New Testament times, so it is probably a word coined by Christians to express God's evenhandedness.

Looking Good

Romans 2:17–29

17 Indeed you are called a Jew, and rest on the law, and make your boast in God,

18 and know His will, and approve the things that are excellent, being instructed out of the law,

19 and are confident that you yourself are a guide to the blind, a light to those who are in darkness,

20 an instructor of the foolish, a teacher of babes, having the form of knowledge and truth in the law.

21 You, therefore, who teach another, do you not teach yourself? You who preach that a man should not steal, do you steal?

22 You who say, "Do not commit adultery," do you commit adultery? You who abhor idols, do you rob temples?

23 You who make your boast in the law, do you dishonor God through breaking the law?

24 For "The name of God is blasphemed among the Gentiles because of you," as it is written.

25 For circumcision is indeed profitable if you keep the law; but if you are a breaker of the law, your circumcision has become uncircumcision.

26 Therefore, if an uncircumcised man keeps the righteous requirements of the law, will not his uncircumcision be counted as circumcision?

27 And will not the physically uncircumcised, if he fulfills the law, judge you who, even with your written code and circumcision, are a transgressor of the law?

28 For he is not a Jew who is one outwardly, nor is that circumcision which is outward in the flesh;

29 but he is a Jew who is one inwardly; and circumcision is that of the heart, in the Spirit, and not in the letter; whose praise is not from men but from God.

An elderly resident in Worcester, Massachusetts, was missing. Her brother said she had gone into a nursing home. When neighbors noticed her mail piling up, they arranged for it to be stopped. Another neighbor paid her grandson to cut the lawn. When they noticed water running out from underneath the door, the utility company was called to shut it off. Finally, the police decide to investigate the house as a possible health hazard. *The Washington Post* reported that the officers were shocked to find the elderly woman's body in the home. Police believed she had died of natural causes four years earlier.

The respectable external appearance of the home covered up what was on the inside. Similarly, many people walk around with the outward appearance of religiosity but are spiritually dead. They make every effort to look good on the outside, but there is no life on the inside. They focus on the externals, such as

a. *Religious heritage* (vv. 17–18). Growing up in a godly home is a wonderful experience. If there was any enviable feature about the Jewish home, it was the fact that usually it was a pious place. Paul says, **Indeed you are called a Jew, and rest on the law, and make your boast in God, and know His will, . . . being instructed out of the law.** Religious instruction in the home gives a child a great advantage, but it does not provide salvation. Someone said, "God has no grandchildren." No matter how well he is taught at home, each person is still responsible for making a personal decision about his relationship with Christ. No one is going to ride into heaven on his parents' or grandparents' coattails.

b. *Religious rules* (vv. 21–24). A businessman well known for his ruthlessness once said to Mark Twain, "Before I die I mean to make a pilgrimage to the Holy Land. I will climb Mount Sinai and read the Ten Commandments aloud at the top." "I have a better idea," Twain replied. "You could stay in Boston and keep them." Hopefully, Twain's retort got the man thinking, but it would have been impossible for him to follow such advice even had he wanted to. The self-deception of the religious person is that he can keep the Law. George Barna reported that six percent of all Americans claim they completely follow each of the Ten Commandments.[18] But Paul says in verses 21 and 22, **You, therefore,**

---

[18] George Barna, *The Barna Report*, (Ventura, California: Gospel Light's Regal Books), 1992–93.

who teach another, do you not teach yourself? You who preach that a man should not steal, do you steal? You who say, "Do not commit adultery," do you commit adultery? You who abhor idols, do you rob temples?** The implied answer is yes. The Law can tell you what to do, but it cannot give you the power to do it.

c. *Religious rituals* (vv. 25–29). For the Jew, one of the most important religious rituals was circumcision. Seven days after the birth of a male child, he was taken to the temple or a priest came to the home and removed the child's foreskin. This was such an important rite that if the day for the circumcision fell on the Sabbath, it was permissible to violate the Sabbath in order to perform this ceremony. Circumcision outwardly indicated that a person was part of God's covenant and God's people. In later times it was believed a necessity for salvation. But Paul says, **For he is not a Jew who is one outwardly, nor is that circumcision which is outward in the flesh; but he is a Jew who is one inwardly, and circumcision is that of the heart, in the Spirit.** Whether we are talking about cutting off part of the body, going to church, being confirmed or giving to meet the budget, such acts may be good but they cannot save us. Religious people need the Savior as much as the pagan or moralist need Him.

CHAPTER 3

The Whole World Condemned
Romans 3:1–31

Paul anticipates that he will have objections, especially from the moralist and the religious people. After all their efforts, is he telling them that they were to no avail? In Romans 3, Paul assures them that, yes, there are advantages, but salvation is not one of them.

Why?

Romans 3:1–8

1 What advantage then has the Jew, or what is the profit of circumcision?

2 Much in every way! Chiefly because to them were committed the oracles of God.

3 For what if some did not believe? Will their unbelief make the faithfulness of God without effect?

4 Certainly not! Indeed, let God be true but every man a liar. As it is written: "That You may be justified in Your words, And may overcome when You are judged."

5 But if our unrighteousness demonstrates the righteousness of God, what shall we say? Is God unjust who inflicts wrath? (I speak as a man.)

6 Certainly not! For then how will God judge the world?

7 For if the truth of God has increased through my lie to

His glory, why am I also still judged as a sinner?
**8 And why not say, "Let us do evil that good may
come"?—as we are slanderously reported and as some affirm
that we say. Their condemnation is just.**

When feeling disappointed, one of the first questions we tend to ask
is *why?* Chuck Swindoll said that the *why* question is usually the one that
hits first and lingers longest.

Those who read Paul's letter to the Romans, especially if they had
attempted to live moral and upright lives, must have wondered, *Why have
I gone to all this effort?* Many people today are asking themselves the
same thing. Paul poses such questions and then answers them.

a. *Why be religious?* (vv. 1–2). Paul asks, **What advantage then has
the Jew, or what is the profit of circumcision?** His response, **Much in
every way!**, is further explained, **Chiefly because to them were
committed the oracles of God.** God chose to commit the reception,
inscription and transmission of His revealed Word to the Jews. That was
no little honor for God's people and no little benefit for all mankind.

A man once asked his pastor, "If there were no heaven, would you
still be a Christian?" "Absolutely," the pastor replied. "By following the
teachings in God's Word I have lived a happier and more fulfilling life
than I ever could have otherwise." Just having the advantage of the
guidance of God's Word makes it worthwhile.

b. *Why be faithful?* (vv. 3–4). The Jews were the keepers of the Old
Testament, but they failed to comprehend its message, especially the
prophetic and messianic passages. Their lack of faith is seen particularly
in their rejection of Jesus as Messiah. The question is, **Will their unbelief
make the faithfulness of God without effect?** Paul's answer is a classic,
Certainly not! God's faithfulness doesn't depend on our faithfulness, but
His fellowship does. The prophet Amos asks, "Can two walk together,
unless they are agreed?" (Amos 3:3). If we choose to go the wrong way,
God will continue on the right way (He will be faithful), but we will not
be walking with Him.

c. *Why be righteous?* (vv. 5–8). **If our unrighteousness
demonstrates the righteousness of God, what shall we say?** This is a

clever but illogical argument. Paul anticipates someone saying (**I speak as a man,** i.e., from a human perspective), "If my unfaithfulness highlights God's faithfulness, is not my sin enhancing the world's concept of God's faithfulness?" In other words, by being bad, I'm making God look good. Therefore my bad is really good.

Paul asks a second question. **Is God unjust who inflicts wrath?** Wouldn't it be unjust of God to punish me for helping to make the picture of His true character more obvious?

Once man sins, he has an amazing ability to rationalize it. Paul says, "I could use that argument myself. You slanderously say I encourage evil If that were true, wouldn't it be good instead of evil as you claim?" It never works to rationalize our sin. How can God forgive us when we are not willing to admit there is anything wrong? Herbert Lockyer, a gifted Bible teacher and preacher, once wrote, "Jesus can save the unholy, the unfit, and the unclean, but the unwilling He cannot save."

Furthermore, faith does not mean that believers can blatantly disregard the moral precepts of the Law. If they do, their actions condemn them, not in the sense of eternal damnation, since believers cannot lose their salvation, but in the sense of revealing the continuing power of sin in their lives. As Paul says, **Their condemnation is just** (i.e., correct or appropriate).

Here Comes the Judge

Romans 3:9–20

9 What then? Are we better than they? Not at all. For we have previously charged both Jews and Greeks that they are all under sin.

10 As it is written: "There is none righteous, no, not one;

11 There is none who understands; There is none who seeks after God.

12 They have all gone out of the way; They have together become unprofitable; There is none who does good, no, not one."

13 "Their throat is an open tomb; With their tongues they have practiced deceit"; "The poison of asps is under their lips";

14 **"Whose mouth is full of cursing and bitterness."**

15 **"Their feet are swift to shed blood;**

16 **Destruction and misery are in their ways;**

17 **And the way of peace they have not known."**

18 **"There is no fear of God before their eyes."**

19 **Now we know that whatever the law says, it says to those who are under the law, that every mouth may be stopped, and all the world may become guilty before God.**

20 **Therefore by the deeds of the law no flesh will be justified in His sight, for by the law is the knowledge of sin.**

J. Willard "Bill" Marriott didn't start the Marriott Corporation from scratch—his father, J. W. Marriott Sr., founded it as a root beer stand in 1927—but he has caused it to grow 20 percent a year for the last decade to more than $7 billion in sales.

He was once asked, "How do you measure your service?" He replied, "We have a program called the 'Phantom Shopper.' An inspector, posing as a customer, visits a unit and rates the service he receives. Then he pulls out his ID card. If the service has been good, he turns over the card and hands the server a $10 bill clipped to the back. If the service is bad, there's no $10 bill. On the card it says, 'Oops!' If someone gets the 'Oops!,' we send him in for retraining.

Paul gives the whole world an "Oops!" To prove that the whole world has rebelled against God and is guilty before the divine judgment bar, the apostle depicts a courtroom in which mankind is on trial. He presents the four components of every judicial procedure: charge, indictment, defense and verdict. Let's enter the courtroom.

a. *The charge* (v. 9). **For we have previously charged**[1] **both Jews and Greeks that they are all under sin**. Paul showed that religious people (like the Jews) are lost because they have not kept the Law, and religious relatives, rules or rituals cannot save them from the

---

[1] The King James Version translates this word as "proved." In the original (Gk: *proaitiaomai*) it is a combination of two Greek words: *pro*, meaning "before," and *altiaomai*, meaning "to bring an accusation against" or "press formal charges." Therefore, a better translation is "charged."

condemnation of disobedience. In addition, he has shown that the heathen are lost because they suppressed God's truth even though they had the witnesses of nature and conscience. He has shown also that the moral man is lost because, though outwardly different from the heathen, inwardly he is guilty of the same sins.

b. *The indictment* (vv. 10–18). Next in the judicial procedure is an indictment. Webster defines an indictment as "a formal written accusation charging one or more persons with the commission of a crime" (*Webster's New World Dictionary*). Although there are 14 individual counts to Paul's indictment of mankind, they can be summarized as follows:

1) *There are none who are righteous* (vv. 9–10). Paul asserts, **There is none righteous, no, not one.** To be **righteous** means "to have a right relationship with God." This "right relationship" is demonstrated by the way we live. In violent streets and broken homes, the cry of anguished souls is not for more laws but for more righteousness.

2) *There are none who understand* (vv. 11–12). The situation grows worse with each charge. Not only are none righteous, **but there is none who understands**. If people understood the serious consequences of their sinful behavior, they surely would abandon it. Instead, Satan has them so securely under his control that sin appears to be pleasurable while God is a wet blanket. When one unbeliever was presented with the opportunity to receive Christ, he responded, "I don't want to give up my fun." He didn't understand his lifestyle was hurting him and his family and eventually would cost him eternal separation from God.

3) *There are none who seek God* (vv. 11–12). Those who have not been quickened by the Holy Spirit have no interest in God. **They have all gone out of the way;**[2] (v. 12). There are only two options in life. Either you walk in God's way or you walk in the world's way. It is impossible to do both.

4) *There are none who do good* (v. 12–20). Some might point at various humanitarian efforts made by unbelievers and feel Paul has gone too far. But goodness goes beyond the act itself and includes the motives.

---

[2] This is used of a camel caravan crossing the desert that has strayed from the route and cannot return to the proper path. Likewise, man has lost his way by deviating from God's prescribed route of righteousness.

Paul would not deny that heathens have done deeds of charity, but they fall short of being "good" because verse 18 says, **There is no fear of God before their eyes**. Their deeds were not done out of a reverence or awe for God but for other reasons. Many people desire to create a memorial for themselves or to receive the praise and admiration of others. Acts committed with these motives are not good.

c. *The defense* (v. 19). In any trial, the accused has the opportunity to make a defense. In this case, however, the proof is so overwhelming **that every mouth may be stopped**. The famous French infidel, Jean Jacques Rousseau, refused to marry his mistress and sent his illegitimate children to an orphanage. When confronted with his behavior he exclaimed: "I will stand before God and defend my conduct!" Bad news for Rousseau. No one will have a defense before the righteous God.

d. *The verdict* (v. 19–20). The charge has been made (all are under sin), the indictment has been read, and no defense can be made. The only step left is the verdict, which is "guilty as charged." Paul concludes **and all the world may become guilty before God**. Furthermore, he says **no flesh will be justified in His sight**. We are hopelessly and helplessly at the mercy of God. We are worthy of His wrath and His judgment. There is only one avenue open before us—and that is to throw ourselves upon the mercy of the court.

The Faith Factor

Romans 3:21–23

21 But now the righteousness of God apart from the law is revealed, being witnessed by the Law and the Prophets,

22 even the righteousness of God which is through faith in Jesus Christ to all and on all who believe. For there is no difference;

23 for all have sinned and fall short of the glory of God,

A few moments spent glancing through the tabloids at the checkout counters of your local grocery store will challenge your faith. Some of the recent headlines include, "Man, 71, Weds 12–Yr–Old Girl," "25 Year Old Trapped in a Baby's Body," and "New Sightings of the Abominable Snow Man."

Compared with what these stories require, the faith that God asks for is relatively simple and placed in a much more reliable Source. It is by faith, Paul says, that we receive our righteousness from God.[3] It is a righteousness:

a. *That can be seen in the Old Testament* (v. 21). God's righteousness is **witnessed by the Law and the Prophets.**[4] God never hid His righteousness. In fact, the purpose of the Law (in particular the Ten Commandments) was to reveal God's righteousness and the futility of man's efforts to achieve that righteousness by keeping the Law (see Ps. 7:9 and Prov. 21:12).

b. *That can be had through Jesus Christ* (v. 22). Paul says this righteousness is **through faith in Jesus Christ.** Where the Old Testament could only show the righteousness of God, in the New Testament, through Jesus Christ, we can actually share in that righteousness with God. When we accept Christ as our Savior, our sins are forgiven and a "right relationship" with God the Father is established.

c. *That is needed by all* (vv. 22–23). Paul doesn't pull any punches. He says, **For there is no difference; for all have sinned and fall short of the glory of God.** Whether Jew or Greek (i.e., non–Jewish or Gentile), we all need God's righteousness. Righteousness is the only gift in the world that fits everybody regardless of size, sex or nationality.

God's Plan

Romans 3:24–31

24 being justified freely by His grace through the redemption that is in Christ Jesus,

---

[3] The apostle begins this section with the Greek phrase *Ti oun*, which is usually translated "but now." The phrase is used in the Pauline Epistles 18 times and twice in Hebrews. It does not occur anywhere else in the New Testament. It is an adverb of time and a favorite expression of Paul when he makes a transition from a dark, gloomy picture to something wonderful that God does for us.

[4] The "Law and the Prophets" indicated all of the Old Testament books, including the poetical books and the historical books, as well as the first 5 books (the Law) and the last 17 books (the prophets).

25 whom God set forth to be a propitiation by His blood, through faith, to demonstrate His righteousness, because in His forbearance God had passed over the sins that were previously committed,

26 to demonstrate at the present time His righteousness, that He might be just and the justifier of the one who has faith in Jesus.

27 Where is boasting then? It is excluded. By what law? Of works? No, but by the law of faith.

28 Therefore we conclude that a man is justified by faith apart from the deeds of the law.

29 Or is He the God of the Jews only? Is He not also the God of the Gentiles? Yes, of the Gentiles also,

30 since there is one God who will justify the circumcised by faith and the uncircumcised through faith.

31 Do we then make void the law through faith? Certainly not! On the contrary, we establish the law.

According to one study only 3 percent of all people have written goals and plans. Another 10 percent have goals and plans but keep them in their head. The rest (87 percent) do not know where they are going.

Fortunately, God has a plan and it is recorded in His Word. Paul reveals three aspects of that plan.

a. *God plans for us to be justified by His grace* (v. 24). Someone said that the word *justify* means "just–as–if–I'd–never–sinned."[5] It is vastly more than being pardoned; it is even greater than being forgiven. You may wrong me and I may say, "I forgive you." But I have not justified you. I cannot justify you. I am unable to pay for your sin. Yet when God justifies a man, He says, "I pronounce you a righteous man. Henceforth I am going to treat you as if you never committed any sin!" He can do that because Christ paid for our sins.

---

[5] *Justify* (Gk: *dikaioumenoi*) literally means "to be declared to be in the right." God does not *make* us right in the sense of being without fault or sin; rather, He declares us to be right based on Christ's death on the cross.

What shocked Paul's fellow Jews was that he claimed God was willing to justify not just the good people (themselves) but sinners! God does not wait for us to clean up our lives before we come to Him; rather, He meets us where we are and takes us to where He wants us to be. This is grace. **We are justified freely by His grace.**

b. *God plans for us to be set free by Christ's blood* (vv. 25–26). Some find the thought of blood disturbing. They want their Gospel spotless and sanitized. They don't want to think about something as messy as blood. But Paul says it is **in Christ Jesus, Whom God set forth to be a propitiation**[6] **by His blood,** that we have righteousness. A lawyer who claimed to be a Christian was asked how he could defend a client whom he knew was guilty. He replied, "Because Someone defended me when I was guilty." But God did more than enable man to escape the consequence of his crime; He took that consequence upon Himself in Christ. Through the blood of Christ, God has done everything that needs to be done—the penalty is paid. It is up to us to receive the saving benefits of His blood.

c. *God plans for us to be humbled by our inadequacies* (vv. 27–31). Paul asks, **Where is boasting then? It is excluded. By what law? Of works? No, but by the law of faith.** Pride is our fatal flaw. Satan appealed to Adam's and Eve's pride by promising them that if they ate the fruit from the tree of the knowledge of good and evil, they would be just like God (Gen. 3:5). Nothing has changed since then. If salvation were a matter of *doing* something, churches would be full. Much of the popularity of the cults comes from their "works" orientation. If we could stand before God and say, "I have done this and this and this; therefore, You should let me into heaven," we would love it! Salvation would be the most popular game around. We could boast, "Look what I have done!" It would appeal to our pride.

But that is not the way it is. There is no room for works or pride or boasting. Instead, humility is required. If we cannot come to God humbly,

---

[6] When the Hebrew Old Testament was translated into Greek (the Septuagint), the word chosen to translate *mercy seat* (Heb: *kaphorah*) was *hilasterion*, which means "the place of propitiation." To propitiate means to appease an offended party, and the *hilasterion* (mercy seat) was where the sins of Israel were atoned by blood. It was here the penalty was paid and the wrath of God (the offended party) was appeased. It is certainly no coincidence that Paul uses the term *mercy seat* to describe Jesus Christ. Christ is our mercy seat. He atoned for our sins, paid our penalty and appeased the offended party. Jesus Christ is where God meets man.

we cannot come to Him at all. Peter says, "God resists the proud, but gives grace to the humble" (1 Pet. 5:5).

CHAPTER 4

The Experienced Traveler
Romans 4:1–25

Getting advice from seasoned travelers is a tremendous help when planning a trip. They often can give you tips that guidebooks leave out.

When Paul spoke of salvation by grace through faith alone, he knew some people would say this was an unexplored and dangerous road. They would caution the apostle against embarking on such a radical journey. But like any wise traveler, Paul turns to those who had taken the trip before him, men like Abraham and David. The Scripture says, "By the mouth of two or three witnesses the matter shall be established" (Deut. 19:15), so Paul appeals to the experiences of these two great saints to prove that salvation by grace through faith is the only route that leads to God.

Is It Faith or Works?

Romans 4:1–8

1 What then shall we say that Abraham our father has found according to the flesh?

2 For if Abraham was justified by works, he has something of which to boast, but not before God.

3 For what does the Scripture say? "Abraham believed God, and it was accounted to him for righteousness."

4 Now to him who works, the wages are not counted as grace but as debt.

5 But to him who does not work but believes on Him who justifies the ungodly, his faith is accounted for righteousness,

6 just as David also describes the blessedness of the man to whom God imputes righteousness apart from works:

7 "Blessed are those whose lawless deeds are forgiven, And whose sins are covered;

8 Blessed is the man to whom the Lord shall not impute sin."

The great Polish astronomer Copernicus died in 1543. Inscribed on his gravestone at the cemetery in Frauenbaerg is this epitaph: "O Lord, the faith Thou didst give to Saint Paul I cannot ask. The mercy Thou didst give to Saint Peter I dare not ask. But Lord, the grace Thou didst give unto the dying robber, that Lord, show to me." Copernicus was an outstanding scientist, but more important, he was a Christian who understood the principle of God's salvation by grace through faith.

Sometimes we have difficulty understanding that we are saved totally apart from works. Attending church, working in a homeless shelter, living a decent life—all are noble, but none of these will save you. Salvation is solely by grace through faith. It is not what you do, but what Jesus did for you at Calvary that makes the difference. Paul lays out a threefold argument as to why this is true:

a. *Salvation by faith is logical* (vv. 1–2). **For if Abraham was justified by works, he has something of which to boast, but not before God.** Works are good. We were saved in order to do good works (Eph. 2:10). But works are the result of salvation, not its means. Good works cannot provide salvation. If we are saved by works, then God is obligated to save us. It is illogical to think that we could work for our salvation and then demand it as payment for what we did. God would never place Himself in a situation where He could be forced to do anything. God will not be a debtor to any man. Either we accept our salvation by grace or it is not available.

b. *Salvation by faith is historical* (vv. 3–5). Paul argues his point from one of the most revered figures in Jewish history, Abraham. How was he saved? **For what does the Scripture say? "Abraham believed**

God and it was accounted[1] to him for righteousness." The Old Testament saints were saved the same way that we are saved today—by believing that God will (Old Testament) and has (Church Age) provided a Savior for our sins. Nothing has changed except for the tense of the verb. One looks forward to the cross; the other looks backward. There is a historical continuity that links both the Old and New Testament to the present age. The great saints of history have always believed this truth. Like Abraham, by believing **on Him who justifies the ungodly,[2] [their] faith is accounted for righteousness.**

c. *Salvation by faith is biblical* (vv. 6–8). Paul appeals to another great Jewish leader, King David. David taught that a person's sins are forgiven by grace. In verses 7–8 Paul quotes Psalm 32:1–2, **"Blessed are those whose lawless deeds are forgiven, and whose sins are covered; blessed is the man to whom the LORD shall not impute sin."** Paul says to the Jews, "Look at your own Scriptures. See for yourself what the Bible teaches. We do not forgive ourselves. We do not cover our own sins. They are forgiven and covered for us, by grace." We should not think this is a new teaching; it is found in the Old Testament from Genesis to Malachi.

Faith Makes a Difference

Romans 4:9–25

9 Does this blessedness then come upon the circumcised only, or upon the uncircumcised also? For we say that faith was accounted to Abraham for righteousness.

10 How then was it accounted? While he was circumcised, or uncircumcised? Not while circumcised, but while uncircumcised.

---

[1] The word translated "accounted" (Gk: *logizomai*) is a commercial term used with regard to credits and debits. It means to set to one's credit or lay to one's charge. If you authorize your lawyer to write checks on your bank account, and he does so, the amount of the check is charged to you, even though he receives the money. The word *logizomai* occurs 11 times in this chapter and is translated by various words such as *count, reckon* and *impute*.

[2] The word that Paul uses for *ungodly* (Gk: *asebes*) is a strong word meaning "an extremely wicked person"—not just sinners in general but very perverse sinners.

11 And he received the sign of circumcision, a seal of the righteousness of the faith which he had while still uncircumcised, that he might be the father of all those who believe, though they are uncircumcised, that righteousness might be imputed to them also,

12 and the father of circumcision to those who not only are of the circumcision, but who also walk in the steps of the faith which our father Abraham had while still uncircumcised.

13 For the promise that he would be the heir of the world was not to Abraham or to his seed through the law, but through the righteousness of faith.

14 For if those who are of the law are heirs, faith is made void and the promise made of no effect,

15 because the law brings about wrath; for where there is no law there is no transgression.

16 Therefore it is of faith that it might be according to grace, so that the promise might be sure to all the seed, not only to those who are of the law, but also to those who are of the faith of Abraham, who is the father of us all

17 (as it is written, "I have made you a father of many nations") in the presence of Him whom he believed, even God, who gives life to the dead and calls those things which do not exist as though they did;

18 who, contrary to hope, in hope believed, so that he became the father of many nations, according to what was spoken, "So shall your descendants be."

19 And not being weak in faith, he did not consider his own body, already dead (since he was about a hundred years old), and the deadness of Sarah's womb.

20 He did not waver at the promise of God through unbelief, but was strengthened in faith, giving glory to God,

21 and being fully convinced that what He had promised He was also able to perform.

22 And therefore "it was accounted to him for righteousness."

23 **Now it was not written for his sake alone that it was imputed to him,**

24 **but also for us. It shall be imputed to us who believe in Him who raised up Jesus our Lord from the dead,**

25 **who was delivered up because of our offenses, and was raised because of our justification.**

A chemist pointed out that if you mix hydrogen and oxygen—the two elements that make up water—you do not get water. In fact, you get no reaction at all. But if you add a small amount of platinum to the mixture, things happen quickly. The oxygen and hydrogen atoms combine and form H_2O.

The same is true spiritually. Our life can interact casually with God and not much happens. But when you add faith, things change quickly. Paul points out that the kind of faith exhibited by Abraham is not content with the status quo. It is a faith that makes a difference.

a. *It is a faith that makes the symbols meaningful* (v. 11). Circumcision was an important symbol to the Jews. It was a mark that identified them as a unique people group. It symbolized their covenant relationship with God. It was so important that, according to Rabbinic tradition, if any Jew was so bad he had to be condemned by God, an angel was appointed to "uncircumcise" him before he entered into punishment.

But Paul claims this symbol took place in Abraham's life at least 14 years after he had been declared righteous.[3] After the birth of Ishmael, **he received the sign of circumcision, a seal of the righteousness of the faith which he had while still uncircumcised.** The sign came *after* the event. In fact, it would have been meaningless unless it represented a reality that had already taken place. Symbols can represent the truth, but they are no substitute for the real thing.

Huddling behind the sign for a storm shelter would offer little protection from an approaching tornado. The value of the sign is to let us know a real storm shelter is nearby. Baptism and communion are like that.

---

[3] Abraham is declared "righteous" in Gen. 15:6 before the birth of Ishmael. Ishmael was 13 years old when he and his father were circumcised (Gen. 17:23–25).

Two symbols common to the Christian faith, they are meaningless without a personal faith in Jesus Christ. Before partaking of the symbol, one has to **walk in the steps of the faith which our father Abraham had while still uncircumcised.**

b. *It is a faith that makes the promises sure* (v. 16). The apostle contends, **Therefore it is of faith that it might be according to grace, so that the promise might be sure to all the seed, not only to those who are of the law, but also to those who are of the faith of Abraham, who is the father of us all.** The word Paul uses for promise means an "unconditional promise."[4] If God's promises were based on works, they would be conditional. Only those who performed at a certain level would receive the promise. This means such extraneous factors as wealth, opportunities and even health would play a role in determining who received the promises. But God's promises are not based on our works. By grace God has determined that only one factor will influence the outcome—faith. Since faith is available to everyone, no one has any more advantage than another. Through faith, the promises surely can be ours.

c. *It is a faith that makes impossible circumstances possible* (v. 19). Circumstances were against Abraham. Both he and Sarah were beyond the age when childbearing was biologically possible. Yet verse 19 says, **And not being weak in faith, he did not consider his own body, already dead (since he was about a hundred years old), and the deadness of Sarah's womb. He did not waver at the promise of God through unbelief but was strengthened in faith, giving glory to God.** In Abraham's eyes, the more difficult the circumstances, the greater the opportunity for God to reveal His power and majesty. Someone has said that when God begins to do a great work, He starts with a great difficulty. Faith enables us to use life's problems as opportunities instead of being defeated by them. We all need that kind of faith!

---

[4] Two Greek words can be translated as promise. *Huposchesis* means a promise that is entered into upon conditions. *Epaggelia* means a promise made out of the goodness of someone's heart with no strings attached. Paul uses the latter word in this verse.

CHAPTER 5

Both Now and Forever
Romans 5:1–21

When it comes to taking trips, there are two kinds of travelers: those who say, "Getting there is half the fun," and those who say, "Getting there is the only fun." The former stops frequently and enjoys the scenery; the latter focuses on the destination and seeks the fastest route to it.

Whether you are primarily concerned with the here and now or prefer to concentrate on what is ahead, Romans 5 has something for you. In Romans 1–3, Paul proves that the whole world stands convicted before God. In Romans 4, he demonstrates that through a faith like Abraham's, it is possible to begin a journey into life. Romans 5 looks more closely at the journey itself. The first 11 verses of this chapter contain two important clauses. In verse 1 the clause is "we have," which is followed by a list of blessings that accompany our journey. In verse 9 the clause is "we shall be," which focuses on the blessings awaiting us when we reach our destination.

Forget Not His Benefits

Romans 5:1–2

1 Therefore, having been justified by faith, we have peace with God through our Lord Jesus Christ,

2 through whom also we have access by faith into this grace in which we stand, and rejoice in hope of the glory of God.

The psalmist admonishes both himself and us, "Bless the LORD, O my soul, and forget not all His benefits" (Ps. 103:2). Unfortunately, we are much better at forgetting than remembering. President Abraham Lincoln told the nation, "We have been the recipients of the choicest bounties of heaven. We have grown in numbers, wealth and power, as no other nation has ever grown. But we have forgotten God."

The tendency to forget is such a common experience that Paul must remind us that our journey into life is not "pie in the sky, by and by." Instead, it has real benefits for us right now, such as

a. *Peace with God* (v. 1). There is little peace in the world. The Stockholm International Peace Research Institute reported 31 wars in 1994. Up to one million civilians were massacred in Rwanda alone during that year.[1] This reflects, however, a far bigger problem: a lack of peace with God. President Herbert Hoover said, "Peace is not made in documents but in the hearts of men." We will never be at peace with one another until we are at peace with God in our hearts.

Verse 1 proclaims, **Therefore, having been justified[2] by faith, we have peace with God through our Lord Jesus Christ.** Jesus makes that peace possible when we accept Him as our Savior. The Greek word translated "with" in this verse can denote a hostile or a friendly relationship. If it is hostile, it is always translated "against." If it is friendly, it is translated "with." This is a friendly relationship. It has not always been that way, but once we are justified—through no effort of our own—God treats us as though we are righteous and declares us to be at peace with Him.

b. *Access to the Father* (v. 2). Once we are justified by faith, we are part of God's family and have the right to come to Him at any time. Paul says, **Through whom also we have access[3] by faith into this grace** (see

---

[1] Associated Press, "31 wars counted in 1994," *The Lincoln Star*, June 15, 1995, p. 3.

[2] The Greek word for "having been justified" is *dikaiothentes*. As an aorist passive participle, it implies an action that took place at a point of time in the past. Furthermore, the subject was acted upon (passive voice) rather than initiating the action. So Paul is saying, "At some definite point in the past, without our help, God declared us righteous (justified) and began to treat us as though we had never sinned. That point, of course, took place when we accepted Christ as our Savior."

also Eph. 2:18). This access to God is not by virtue of our own goodness but by His grace. As Ron Dunn remarks, "The throne room is not sprinkled with the sweat of our activity, but it's sprinkled with the blood of His sacrifice."[4] God is more accessible to us than is the president of the United States. On several occasions I have called the White House in Washington, D.C., but I have never gotten through to speak with the president. How different it is with God. We can actually enter the Father's throne room to speak to Him at any time. Such access, however, came at an enormously high price. It cost Him His Son. To the unbeliever, God appears to be as inaccessible as the president of the United States, but to those who have put their trust in Christ, He is only a prayer away.

c. *Standing before God* (v. 2). Throughout the Bible, the question is raised, "How can sinners stand before a holy God?" Psalm 130:3 says, "If You, LORD, should mark iniquities, O Lord, who could stand?" The implied answer is, "No one." Asaph asks in Psalm 76:7, "You, Yourself, are to be feared; and who may stand in Your presence when once You are angry?" The final book of the Bible says,

> And the kings of the earth, the great men, the rich men, the commanders, the mighty men, every slave and every free man, hid themselves in the caves and in the rocks of the mountains, and said to the mountains and rocks, "Fall on us and hide us from the face of Him who sits on the throne and from the wrath of the Lamb! For the great day of His wrath has come, and who is able to stand?" (Rev. 6:15–17)

God is angry at our sins, and we sin every day. Therefore, who can stand in His presence? Only those who have been justified by the blood of Christ through faith. Paul says that by faith we have a grace **in which**

---

3 *Access* (Gk: *prosagogen*) appears only three times in the New Testament (Rom. 5:2; Eph. 2:18 and 3:12). It literally means "an approach." If you can imagine a super-fast highway (like the autobahn in Germany), you realize how difficult it would be to merge into the traffic without slowing it down. To deal with that problem, approach–ramps have been built long enough to give drivers time to get up to speed before they enter the mainstream of traffic. Jesus Christ is like an approach–ramp. He enables us to "get up to speed" with God.

4 Ron Dunn, *Don't Just Stand There—Pray Something*, (San Bernardino, Calif: Here's Life Publishers), p. 47.

we stand. Robert Haldane, a nineteenth century Scottish pastor in Geneva, Switzerland, wrote, "And it is by Him they enter into the state of grace, so by Him they stand in it, accepted before God, secured, according to His everlasting covenant that they shall not be cast down, but they are fixed in this state of perfect acceptance conferred by sovereign grace, brought into it by unchangeable love and kept in it by the power of a faithful God."[5]

     d. *Hope in the glory of God* (v. 2). A day is coming when the glory of God will be revealed. His power and majesty will subdue the world, and every knee shall bow and every tongue confess that Jesus Christ is Lord (Phil. 2:10–11). That is our hope.[6] Everything we have gone through—the trials we have faced, the ridicule we have experienced, the misunderstandings we have borne for the sake of Christ—will be made right. Therefore, we **rejoice in hope of the glory of God**.

Many years ago a submarine was rammed by another ship and quickly sank off the Massachusetts coast. A diver was sent down to see if anyone had survived even though rescue was impossible. When the diver placed his helmeted head against the side of the submarine, he could hear someone tapping out by Morse code the question, "Is—there—any—hope?" Sadly, the diver tapped the reply, "Hope—in—God—alone." Ultimately, that is where all hope lies for everyone. While others see only a hopeless end, Christians see an endless hope.

Glory in Tribulation

Romans 5:3–5

    3 And not only that, but we also glory in tribulations, knowing that tribulation produces perseverance;

    4 and perseverance, character; and character, hope.

    5 Now hope does not disappoint, because the love of God has been poured out in our hearts by the Holy Spirit who was given to us.

---

[5] Robert Haldane, *Exposition of the Epistle of the Romans*, (London: Banner of Truth), p. 186.

[6] In the biblical sense, *hope* always means "a sure expectation."

One of my favorite children's books is *Alexander and the Terrible, Horrible, No Good, Very Bad Day*. Unfortunately, it's too long to share in its entirety, but it begins like this:

> I went to sleep with gum in my mouth and now there's gum in my hair. When I got out of bed, I tripped on my skateboard and by mistake dropped my sweater in the sink while the water was running. And I could tell it was going to be a horrible, terrible, no good, very bad day.
>
> At breakfast, Anthony found a Corvette Stingray car kit in his breakfast cereal. And Nick found a Junior Undercover Agent code ring in his breakfast cereal. But in my breakfast cereal box, all I found was breakfast cereal. I think I'll move to Australia.[7]

Poor Alexander's day never improved. He had a terrible day at school. He had a horrible time at the dentist's office after school. When finally he got ready for bed, his Mickey Mouse night-light burned out, and the cat wanted to sleep with Anthony instead of him. Then he knew that he had had a terrible, horrible, no good, very bad day.

Some people not only have bad days like Alexander, but bad weeks or bad months. A few seem to go through their whole life beset by trials. What do these people do? Paul counsels to **glory in tribulations** (v. 3) and then gives the reasons why:

a. *Tribulation produces perseverance* (v. 3). Perseverance is developed only when we face and overcome trials that tempt us to give up. When Wilma Rudolph was a young child she had polio. The disease left her with a crooked left leg. In spite of that handicap she wanted to run. At age 12 she began to overcome her physical disability. By the time she was in high school, she was outrunning all the other girls. In 1956 she ran in the Olympics in Melbourne, Australia, and won a bronze medal. In 1960, at the Rome Olympics, she won three gold medals. It was tribulation that gave her the opportunity to learn the perseverance needed to win. The journey into life is a marathon, not a sprint. We need the perseverance that comes through tribulation.

---

[7] Judith Viorst, *Alexander and the Terrible, Horrible, No Good, Very Bad Day* (New York: Atheneum, 1972).

b. *Perseverance produces character* (v. 4). Someone once said that our reputation is what people think we are; our character is what God knows we are. Character is what we are when all the outer trappings are stripped away. God considers our character more important than our comfort. Our character is shaped and molded as we persevere through trials and tests. God loves us so much that He would rather allow pain to create in us a godly character than permit comfort to cause us to go to wrack and ruin.

c. *Character produces hope* (v. 4). A godly character has confidence in the workings of God. The person who has been through the trials that develop such a character has seen God transform disasters into delights and gloominess into glory many times. He has learned to trust God for the outcome. On May 17, 1987, two Iraqi missiles struck the *USS Stark* while it was on patrol in the Persian Gulf. The incident left 37 seamen dead. In an interview with reporters, Barbara Kiser, wife of one of the sailors killed, said there was no need to mourn because "God doesn't make mistakes." That kind of hope comes only with godly character.

d. *Hope produces love* (v. 5). Paul says **the love of God has been poured out in our hearts**. This is not our love for others (although it results in that) but the realization of God's love for us. The instrument for this love is none other than the Holy Spirit, **who was given to us**. When we pass through the trials and discover the certainties of God's promises, we cannot fail to realize how much our Father loves us.

Show Me

Romans 5:6–8

⁶ **For when we were still without strength, in due time Christ died for the ungodly.**

⁷ **For scarcely for a righteous man will one die; yet perhaps for a good man someone would even dare to die.**

⁸ **But God demonstrates His own love toward us, in that while we were still sinners, Christ died for us.**

In the musical *My Fair Lady*, Eliza meets a young man, Freddy, who falls in love with her. Daily he writes notes of endearment. Eliza's response to his letters is a cry of frustration:

> Words! Words! I'm so sick of words! . . .
> Don't talk of stars
> Burning above,
> If you're in love,
> Show me!
> Don't talk of love lasting through time.
> Make me no undying vow.
> Show me now!

In the Bible God speaks of His love, but even more, He shows it. Paul says, **But God *demonstrates* His own love toward us** (italics mine). God's love is not something we only hear about; it is something we experience right now. His love is

a. *Timely* (v. 6). At just the right time (or as Paul says, **in due time**), Christ died for the ungodly. It is possible for us to do the right thing at the wrong time, but not God. He has a plan that was plotted before the foundations of the world (Eph. 1:4), and it adheres to a strict time schedule. God is never a moment too early or a moment too late. At the right time His Son was born into the world (Gal. 4:4); at the right time He died for the world; and at the right time He will return to the world. We can be certain that at the right time God will deal with our situation as well.

b. *Unconditional* (vv. 7–8). The most amazing part of the story of salvation is that Christ died for us while **we were still sinners**. God willingly meets us where we are. He does not demand we clean up our lives before we come to Him. He knows our weaknesses and frailties and accepts us in them.

c. *Sacrificial* (v. 8). But such love demands a price—Christ died for us. He did not simply live a good life; He died. *USA Today* reported that Mother Teresa said to a group preparing to join her order, the Society of the Missionaries of Charity, "Love, to be real, must cost. It must hurt. It must empty us of self."[8] God met those requirements to the degree no one else ever has.

---

[8] *Associated Press, USA Today*, November 17, 1986.

Plus Ultra

Romans 5:9–11

9 Much more then, having now been justified by His blood, we shall be saved from wrath through Him.

10 For if when we were enemies we were reconciled to God through the death of His Son, much more, having been reconciled, we shall be saved by His life.

11 And not only that, but we also rejoice in God through our Lord Jesus Christ, through whom we have now received the reconciliation.

Before Columbus discovered America, Spanish coins carried the Latin inscription *Ne Plus Ultra*, which means "no more beyond." After the famous explorer returned with his account of lands and people beyond the human horizon, new coins were made that read, *Plus Ultra*, or, "more beyond."

No list of the benefits of being justified by God would be complete without a mention of those yet to come. Paul assures us there is "more beyond":

a. *We shall escape from God's wrath* (v. 9). Some prefer to focus on God's love and deny that He is a God of wrath. Unwittingly, they are destroying the truth they seek to guard. How could a husband say he loved his wife if he failed to demonstrate his wrath toward an intruder who threatened to harm her? God's wrath is directed at sin because it harms that which He values most—people. Because man has chosen to allow sin to take up residence in himself, he also falls under the condemnation of divine wrath. A day is coming when the full wrath of God will vent itself upon sin and sinner alike. Yet Paul says those for whom Christ died **shall be saved from wrath**.

According to legend, a king was much harassed by a rebellious group in his kingdom. He decreed that every rebel must die. Yet a day came when the rebels stood before him, laid down their weapons and begged for peace. As he was granting their wish one of his advisors said, "But, Sire, you said every rebel must die!" "That is true," replied the king, "but I see no rebels here." Where sin is forgiven; there is no wrath.

b. *We shall be saved by His life* (v. 10). Salvation is usually considered a past event. It took place when we trusted Christ as our Savior. But in a very real sense, it is also future. Paul assures the Philippians, "Being confident of this very thing, that He who has begun a good work in you will complete it until the day of Jesus Christ" (Phil. 1:6). The word *complete* has the sense of "no parts missing." Right now there are parts missing in our salvation. Paul reminds us later in this epistle that even creation "groans and labors with birth pangs together until now" and that we also are "eagerly waiting for the adoption, the redemption of our body" (Rom. 8:22–23). Granted, we are saved and our eternal destiny is sealed, but we still await the completion of our salvation, when we will be reunited with our loved ones (1 Thess. 4:17) and given glorified bodies (1 Cor. 15:42–43, 51–53). There will be no more tears or pain, sorrow or sickness, "for the former things have passed away" (Rev. 21:4).

c. *We shall rejoice forever* (v. 11). Paul says **we have now received the reconciliation.**[9] Some years ago the Prince of Wales visited New Delhi, the capital city of India. Waiting for him were 10,000 outcasts under a banner proclaiming "The Prince of the Outcasts." What an appropriate title for Christ. We who have been separated from God, aliens and outcasts, are now reunited with Him through Jesus. We can look forward to the joy of eternally basking in His love and good pleasure. Only in Him do we experience what it is like to be completely known, loved and accepted. Our journey into life has just begun; we are moving toward an exciting journey's end.

Much More

Romans 5:12–21

12 Therefore, just as through one man sin entered the world, and death through sin, and thus death spread to all men, because all sinned—

13 (For until the law sin was in the world, but sin is not

---

[9] The noun and two verbs that express the idea of reconciliation are used only by Paul. Reconciliation signifies a new stage in a relationship that was previously hostile in mind, resulting in estrangement, but which has now been put away in some decisive act (Alan Richardson, *A Theological Word Book of the Bible*, p. 185).

imputed when there is no law.

14 Nevertheless death reigned from Adam to Moses, even over those who had not sinned according to the likeness of the transgression of Adam, who is a type of Him who was to come.

15 But the free gift is not like the offense. For if by the one man's offense many died, much more the grace of God and the gift by the grace of the one Man, Jesus Christ, abounded to many.

16 And the gift is not like that which came through the one who sinned. For the judgment which came from one offense resulted in condemnation, but the free gift which came from many offenses resulted in justification.

17 For if by the one man's offense death reigned through the one, much more those who receive abundance of grace and of the gift of righteousness will reign in life through the One, Jesus Christ.)

18 Therefore, as through one man's offense judgment came to all men, resulting in condemnation, even so through one Man's righteous act the free gift came to all men, resulting in justification of life.

19 For as by one man's disobedience many were made sinners, so also by one Man's obedience many will be made righteous.

20 Moreover the law entered that the offense might abound. But where sin abounded, grace abounded much more,

21 so that as sin reigned in death, even so grace might reign through righteousness to eternal life through Jesus Christ our Lord.

A little boy once said, "When mom makes me a peanut butter sandwich, I know she loves me. When she puts jam with the peanut butter, I know she really loves me!" The truths Paul shares in these closing verses of chapter five imply that God "really loves us." He does more than hand us a peanut butter sandwich—He puts the jam on it. Three times in verses

15–20 Paul repeats the phrase "much more." As terrible and destructive as sin is, the good we receive from Christ is "much more":

a. *Christ's gift is much more than Adam's penalty* (v. 15). When Adam rebelled, **sin entered the world and death through sin** (v. 12). Even before the Law was given, which spelled out man's sin, humans experienced the penalty of Adam's sin because all sinned[10] (vv. 13–14). Christ's death on the cross, however, paid the penalty for sin and gave us life. But we have much more. John says that Christ came that we might have life and have it abundantly (John 10:10)—not just an ordinary life, but an overflowing, supernaturally charged and exuberant life able to **abound to many**.

b. *Christ's reign is much more than Adam's kingdom* (v. 17). When Adam was created, he was given "dominion over the fish of the sea, over the birds of the air, and over the cattle, over all the earth and over every creeping thing that creeps on the earth" (Gen. 1:26). He was told to "be fruitful and multiply; fill the earth and subdue it; have dominion over the fish of the sea, over the birds of the air, and over every living thing that moves on the earth" (v. 28). When Adam sinned, he lost for himself and all his posterity the right to rule over creation. Instead God said, "In the sweat of your face you shall eat bread till you return to the ground" (3:19). In place of Adam's earthly rule, however, Christ gives us a spiritual kingdom. We will **reign in life through the One, Jesus Christ** (v. 17). While all the details remain to be seen, Scripture still makes it clear that we will rule with Christ (2 Tim. 2:12; Rev. 1:6; 5:10; 20:4–6). The kingdom gained through Christ's righteousness is "much more" than that which was lost by Adam's sin.

---

[10] The theological term for this is *imputation*. It means "to charge to one's account." For example, if someone from your family charges something on your credit card, you are responsible. Someone else buys, but you pay. The same principle is true spiritually. Adam's sin in the Garden of Eden is charged to your account. He acted as your representative and did what you would have done. The good news is that Christ's righteousness works the same way. When Christ, our sinless Savior, died on the cross, He reversed what Adam had done. His payment for sin is charged to our account and balances out the debt of sin when we have saving faith in Him.

c. *Christ's grace is much more than sin's condemnation* (v. 20). The depravity of sin is almost inestimable. In fact, there is only one thing greater than man's sin—God's grace. Paul reminds us, **where sin abounded, grace abounded much more**. No matter how big our sin, God's grace is even bigger. God has forgiven murderers (Moses), liars (Abraham) and adulterers (David). He can certainly forgive you.

CHAPTER 6

The Journey Continues

Romans 6:1–23

An old Chinese proverb says, "The journey of a thousand miles begins with just one step." Of course, to complete that journey one must take many more steps. The journey into life has many steps. Thus far we have taken two. The first step was to realize that we are condemned sinners. Paul establishes this condemnation in 1:18–3:23. The key verse is Romans 1:18: **For the wrath of God is revealed from heaven against all ungodliness and unrighteousness of men, who suppress the truth in unrighteousness.** The second step was to realize that God has provided a way out of this condemnation through Jesus Christ. When we trusted Christ as our Savior we were justified. Justification was discussed in 3:24–5:21. The key verse is Romans 3:24: **being justified freely by His grace through the redemption that is in Christ Jesus.** Now, beginning with Romans 6, we add a third step—sanctification.

In chapter 6, Paul contrasts sanctification with justification. Basically, justification deals with the penalty for sin, which is death (Rom. 6:23). God justifies us on the basis of faith in Christ. It doesn't mean that we are pure and never sin, but it does mean that Christ's righteousness is credited to our account. We do nothing for our justification. We are simply declared to be righteous at a point in time and treated from then on as if we were. Through justifcation we are delivered from the penalty of death.

Sanctification, on the other hand, deals with the power of sin—what sin does in our life. Both justification and sanctification are works of God, but sanctification is a progressive act of God.

Paul draws other contrasts as well. Justification deals with the unsaved sinner, while sanctification deals with the saved sinner. The end result of justification is our salvation. The end result of sanctification is obedience.

The Unthinkable

Romans 6:1–2

1 What shall we say then? Shall we continue in sin that grace may abound?

2 Certainly not! How shall we who died to sin live any longer in it?

On April 19, 1995, at 9:02 a.m. the unthinkable happened. A van loaded with explosives was detonated while parked in front of the Alfred P. Murrah Federal Building in Oklahoma City, Oklahoma. The ensuing blast demolished the front half of the building, killing 168 people. Nineteen of these were children attending a day care center on the first floor. Americans reacted with horror and shock. How could anyone even contemplate an outrage like this? Only someone with deep emotional problems would consider committing such a crime.

Paul is equally shocked that some Christians were saying, "All right, I'm saved. Now I can live in sin and give God the opportunity to demonstrate even more grace than before." Paul indignantly replies, **Certainly not!** Only someone with deep spiritual problems would even consider such an attitude.

Unfortunately, such unthinkables do happen—possibly for the following reasons:

a. *A misunderstanding of sin.* Many Christians do not understand what sin is. They have a worldly view of right and wrong. In the mid–1980s *People* magazine took a poll of a large number of its readers. The poll asked individuals to rank in degree of "sinfulness" a list of 50 items. Understandably, murder was listed first most often. Second was rape, then incest, child abuse and spying against one's country. After these top five, however, the rankings reflect a flagrant misconception of sin. For example, number 40 on the list was living together without marriage, and 42 was premarital sex. Items considered by the majority as more sinful than these included parking in a handicap zone (23) and cutting into line (28). If people believe that parking in a handicap zone or cutting into line is more sinful than an illicit relationship, then they do not understand what the Bible teaches about sin.

b. *A lack of accountability.* People live under the false assumption that they do not have to be responsible for their actions. Some years ago columnist Bob Greene blamed the world's troubles on what he calls the "death of the permanent record." In years past the "permanent record" hung over every school child's head like a cloud. If he misbehaved, the teacher would threaten to record it in his permanent record, where it would follow him for the rest of his scholastic career. This intimidation usually brought the desired repentance. Today, however, a child would probably file suit under the Freedom of Information Act, gain possession of his files and have them wiped clean before recess. Where such an attitude prevails, people think they can get away with anything. Little does our world realize that God keeps a record. Revelation 20:12 says, "And I saw the dead, small and great, standing before God, and books were opened. And another book was opened, which is the Book of Life. And the dead were judged according to their works, by the things which were written in the books." There is still a permanent record, and only the blood of Christ can expunge these books.

c. *A twisted kind of logic.* Others have a perverted view of how sin may enhance the image of God. They argue that since their sinning gives God the opportunity to show His graciousness, the more they sin, the better God looks in forgiving them their trespasses. But this takes advantage of God's grace. If we are to accept the blood of Jesus Christ as atonement for our sins, we must take seriously the admonition to live righteously in a crooked and perverse world (Phil. 2:15).

This I Know

Romans 6:3–11

3 Or do you not know that as many of us as were baptized into Christ Jesus were baptized into His death?

4 Therefore we were buried with Him through baptism into death, that just as Christ was raised from the dead by the glory of the Father, even so we also should walk in newness of life.

5 For if we have been united together in the likeness of His death, certainly we also shall be in the likeness of His resurrection,

6 knowing this, that our old man was crucified with Him, that the body of sin might be done away with, that we should no longer be slaves of sin.

7 For he who has died has been freed from sin.

8 Now if we died with Christ, we believe that we shall also live with Him,

9 knowing that Christ, having been raised from the dead, dies no more. Death no longer has dominion over Him.

10 For the death that He died, He died to sin once for all; but the life that He lives, He lives to God.

11 Likewise you also, reckon yourselves to be dead indeed to sin, but alive to God in Christ Jesus our Lord.

The late Paul Little frequently used an illustration in his classes on evangelism of a man with a fried egg hanging on his ear. This man told everyone he met how the fried egg gave him peace, joy and comfort. How could you argue with that? You cannot deny a person's feelings—only his facts.

Some Christians approach sanctification the same way. If they are doing well, they feel sanctified. If they are struggling, they feel their sanctification has suffered a setback. In truth, sanctification is not based on either doing *or* feeling. It is based on fact. We need to *know* what Christ has done for us when we accept Him into our lives. That is why

Paul records in verses 3–11 four facts we need to know about our life after we trust Christ as our Savior:

a. *We have a new family history* (v. 3–5). If you adopt a child, your history becomes that child's. If your grandfather is a horse thief, that child's great-grandfather is a horse thief. The child may not like it; he may be embarrassed by it; nevertheless, it is true. When we trust Christ, we also are adopted into God's family (Rom. 8:15). But we are not only placed into God's family, we are placed "in Christ."[1] That means every part of Christ's life becomes a part of our life, including His death and resurrection. Paul says, **Therefore we were buried with Him through baptism into death, that just as Christ was raised from the dead by the glory of the Father, even so we also should walk in newness of life. For if we have been united together in the likeness of His death, certainly we also shall be in the likeness of His resurrection** (Rom. 6:4–5). Our past is replaced by Christ's past in God's eyes.

b. *We have a new life to live* (v. 4). In 2 Corinthians 5:17 Paul says we are "new creatures" (some translations say, "new creations") in Christ. Because the sin debt is paid, **we also should walk in newness of life**. Some years ago Mississippi had a financial problem. In 1841 the state borrowed $7 million from France, and now that debt was being called in. With interest the loan had grown to about $50 million. The state defaulted, but the comment was made, "These European bankers never forget." Fortunately, God does.[2] We need to know that when we accept Christ as Savior, our sins are cast as far as the East is from the West and we begin a new life.

c. *We have a new freedom from sin* (vv. 6–7). Sin no longer has power over us as it once did. Unbelievers are in bondage to sin and will naturally sin. For a Christian, however, **our old man[3] was crucified with Him, that**

---

[1] The expression "in Christ" occurs 87 times in the New Testament.

[2] When we say God forgets, we do not mean He has a faulty memory. The word *forget* has a variety of meanings in Scripture. When used of God it means that He does not remember with the purpose of avenging Himself against us. Jesus paid it all.

[3] The expression "old man" refers to our old self—the person we once were before we were saved. When Christ died for us, we died with Him. This crucifixion is not a daily experience but a past experience, expressed by the aorist tense in Greek. Christ now lives His life through us (Gal. 2:20).

the body of sin might be done away with, that we should no longer be slaves of sin. We do not have two "selfs" struggling within us, but we do have old thought patterns and sinful habits that encourage us to behave as we did when our old nature was in charge. The Bible calls this the "flesh" (Gal. 5:17). As believers we are not controlled by sin; we choose to sin.

d. *We have a new attitude toward death* (vv. 8–11). The unsaved person lives in fear of death. He may call it a "survival instinct," but in essence it is fear. People will do almost anything to stay alive. Satan has used this fear to control the human race and keep it in bondage (Heb. 2:15). Christ's resurrection, however, proves that we need not fear death. Death is not the dreaded end that Satan portrays it as; rather, it is a new beginning for those who belong to Christ. This breaks the power that fear has had over us. **Death no longer has dominion over Him** (Christ) or us.

Dealing With Sin

Romans 6:12–14

12 Therefore do not let sin reign in your mortal body, that you should obey it in its lusts.

13 And do not present your members as instruments of unrighteousness to sin, but present yourselves to God as being alive from the dead, and your members as instruments of righteousness to God.

14 For sin shall not have dominion over you, for you are not under law but under grace.

One of the strangest places I have visited is a monastery located southeast of Bethlehem in the hill country of Judea, in the middle of nowhere. Few people visit Mar Saba, and no women are allowed. Even your baggage is checked just to make sure nothing sinful enters in. The monastery is inhabited by a group of monks who live apart from the world to try to keep sin in check. These men are very sincere about what they are doing—but they are sincerely wrong. Isolation is not the answer. Instead, Paul says

a. *Choose to avoid sin* (v. 12). As we said earlier, non–Christians do

80

not commit sin by choice but by nature. They *are* sinners. On the other hand, Paul instructs Christians, **Therefore do not let sin reign in your mortal body**. This implies that a Christian can and should avoid sin. He is freed from the power of sin but still has the option to choose it. The best response to this temptation is to follow Paul's advice to Timothy: "Flee also youthful lusts; but pursue righteousness, faith, love, peace with those who call on the Lord out of a pure heart" (2 Tim. 2:22). Wherever sin is, that is where we should not be. The goal is to stay away from sin—not see how close we can get to it.

A wealthy man was hiring a chauffeur. As each candidate came in, he asked them one question, "How close do you think you could drive to a 50-foot drop-off?" The first prospective employee said, "I could drive within one foot." The next applicant said, "I could drive within six inches." The last job seeker replied, "Sir, I'd stay as far away from that drop-off as I could." Guess who got the job!

As Robert Orben wryly remarked, "Many people pray to be delivered from temptation, but still want to 'keep in touch.'" This is an unwise practice for Christians.

b. *Do what is right* (v. 13). Not only should we avoid what is wrong, we also need to actively pursue what is right. We can sometimes be like the little girl who stamped her feet and screamed, "I won't! I won't! I won't!" But no one ever found out what she would. Paul says to **present yourselves to God as being alive from the dead, and your members as instruments of righteousness to God.** Find something good to do—and do it.

c. *Reckon with reality* (v. 14). When Adam sinned, he turned the control of his life over to Satan. Sin had dominion over him. He was a slave to unrighteousness. When we accept Christ as our Savior, the power of sin and the authority of Satan in our lives are overthrown. The Law, which condemns us, is replaced by grace, which saves us. But Satan does not want us to know that. He wants us to live as though we were under the old system. Paul says, "Face reality, folks. **For sin shall not have dominion over you, for you are not under law but under grace.**" Occasionally you'll see a sign in a restaurant that says, "Under new management." The implied message is, "Hey, we're different now. Whatever your experience with us has been in the past, we've changed.

Come in and give us a try!" In the same way, we could say when we accept Christ, "We're under new management. We've changed. We are no longer under law but grace." Let's live that way!

A Little Plant Called Sin

Romans 6:15–23

15 What then? Shall we sin because we are not under law but under grace? Certainly not!

16 Do you not know that to whom you present yourselves slaves to obey, you are that one's slaves whom you obey, whether of sin to death, or of obedience to righteousness?

17 But God be thanked that though you were slaves of sin, yet you obeyed from the heart that form of doctrine to which you were delivered.

18 And having been set free from sin, you became slaves of righteousness.

19 I speak in human terms because of the weakness of your flesh. For just as you presented your members as slaves of uncleanness, and of lawlessness leading to more lawlessness, so now present your members as slaves of righteousness for holiness.

20 For when you were slaves of sin, you were free in regard to righteousness.

21 What fruit did you have then in the things of which you are now ashamed? For the end of those things is death.

22 But now having been set free from sin, and having become slaves of God, you have your fruit to holiness, and the end, everlasting life.

23 For the wages of sin is death, but the gift of God is eternal life in Christ Jesus our Lord.

A little plant called the sundew grows in the Australian bush country. It is a delicate-looking plant with a slender stem and tiny, round leaves fringed with hairs that glisten with bright drops of liquid as fine as dew. But any insect that dares to draw close should beware, for while its clusters of red, white and pink blossoms are harmless, the leaves are deadly. The shiny moisture on each leaf is sticky and will trap any bug that touches it. The struggle to get free is futile. In fact, movement of the insect causes the leaves to close even more tightly around it. This innocent-looking plant actually feeds upon its victims if they do not quickly wriggle out of the entanglement.

Sin is the same way. It promises joy and freedom but does not deliver them. Instead, sin results in

a. *A downward trend* (v. 19). Sin always leads downward. Someone pointed out that when Jonah rebelled against God, he went down to Joppa (Jon. 1:3), down into the ship (v. 3), down into the ocean (v. 15) and down into the belly of the great fish (v. 17). Paul makes this same point. Sin results in further sinfulness. Verse 19 says, **lawlessness leading to more lawlessness.** You cannot overcome sin by engaging in more sin. No one ever cured drunkenness by drinking—it only gets worse. Without Christ, the only direction possible is down.

b. *Shameful behavior* (v. 21). People who have not seared their conscience and are still able to look objectively at their actions while under the influence of alcohol or drugs will openly admit their behavior is shameful. While the locker rooms of America may be filled with the boasts of sexual conquests, doctors offices are filled with people shamed by the sexually transmitted diseases passed on by these behaviors. When we become Christians, we cannot change past behavior or the consequences of the things we have done, but in Christ, we can be forgiven and released from the shame.

c. *Eternal death* (vv. 16, 23). *Death* sometimes refers to our physical body, but the Bible also uses this term to describe a separation from God. Since sin and God cannot coexist, one of them must go. If we choose to keep our sin, then we will be eternally separated from God. If we choose God, our sins can be dealt with through Jesus Christ, and nothing can ever tear us away from the love of God. While death is the wages we earn, we can choose to quit the devil before payday.

CHAPTER 7

The Law
Romans 7:1–25

As you travel throughout the United States, you will see signs that say, "Buckle Up—It's the Law." No questions asked; no options given. It's the law. This aptly describes man's relationship with God throughout the Old Testament period. People were under the Law—no questions asked; no options given. It was literally "do or die." When Christ came, however, the situation changed. His death on the cross turned our relationship from one of "do or die" to "look and live." Paul wants his readers to understand that we have a completely different relationship with God—one of grace, not Law.

From Law to Love

Romans 7:1–6

1 Or do you not know, brethren (for I speak to those who know the law), that the law has dominion over a man as long as he lives?

2 For the woman who has a husband is bound by the law to her husband as long as he lives. But if the husband dies, she is released from the law of her husband.

3 So then if, while her husband lives, she marries another man, she will be called an adulteress; but if her husband dies, she is free from that law, so that she is no adulteress, though she has married another man.

4 Therefore, my brethren, you also have become dead to the law through the body of Christ, that you may be married

to another; even to Him who was raised from the dead, that we should bear fruit to God.

5 For when we were in the flesh, the passions of sins which were aroused by the law were at work in our members to bear fruit to death.

6 But now we have been delivered from the law, having died to what we were held by, so that we should serve in the newness of the Spirit and not in the oldness of the letter.

Oliver Wendell Holmes, perhaps the greatest of all jurists in United States history, wrote, "The values of a reasonably just society will reflect themselves in a reasonably just law. The worse the society, the more law there will be. In hell there will be nothing but law, and due process will be meticulously observed. The better the society, the less law there will be. In heaven there will be no law, and the lion will lie down with the lamb."

The more sin in a society, the more need for law. The more love in society, the less need for law. This is the transition that every Christian makes when he receives Christ as his Savior.

If you want to travel the journey into life successfully, do not look to the Law. The Lord Jesus has provided a new and better way, a way based on love, not law. This new way is

a. *Legitimate* (vv. 1–4). Experienced travelers know that when they go from one country to another they have to go through customs. This usually requires that they declare the contents of their baggage, have their passports stamped and sometimes give proof of their vaccinations, immunizations, etc. If they do not follow these requirements, they are considered illegal aliens and subject to arrest and deportation.

Paul assures us that our transition from Law to love is legal. Using the analogy of marriage, he says, **For the woman who has a husband is bound by the law to her husband as long as he lives. But if the husband dies, she is released from the law of her husband** (v. 2). It is not Paul's intent here to advance the biblical teaching about marriage and divorce. In passing, however, the apostle does reiterate the "till death do us part" quality to marriage (cf. Gen. 2:22–24; Matt. 19:3–9). He then goes on to point out, **So then if, while her husband lives, she marries another man, she will be called an adulteress; but if her husband dies, she is free from** that law, so that she is no adulteress, though she has married another man. Therefore, my brethren, you also have become dead to the law through the body of Christ, that you may be married to another, even to Him who was raised from the dead (vv. 3–4). We are not slipping across the border into this new relationship with Christ as illegal aliens. We have gone through all the proper channels. We never have to worry about being deported because in Christ we have met all the requirements.

b. *Fruitful* (vv. 4–5). Bearing fruit is a sign that we are living in an entirely new relationship. As Dorothy says to her dog, Toto, "I've a feeling we're not in Kansas anymore!" In our old relationship under the Law, the only fruit we could bear was the **fruit to death** (v. 5). Sin and guilt controlled our lives because, while the Law could tell us the kind of fruit we ought to bear, it was powerless to help us produce it. Under the control of the Spirit, however, Galatians 5:22–23 says we can bear such fruit as "love, joy, peace, longsuffering, kindness, goodness, faithfulness, gentleness, self-control. Against such there is no law."

c. *Purposeful* (v. 6). One of the most difficult feelings many older people have to overcome is a sense of uselessness. Many have built their lives around their family, but the children are now grown and do not seem to need them anymore. Others have invested their lives in their jobs, but now they are retired and no longer have the satisfaction of their work. But Paul says we can still serve Christ in the newness of the Spirit. Spirit–filled service is not only a privilege, it is something we never outlive. Just ask Gladys Stall of Lake Magdalene, Florida, who has taught Sunday school for 82 years. She began at the age of 14 and is still teaching six- and seven-year-olds at the age of 96. The psalmist says, "Those who are planted in the house of the LORD shall flourish in the courts of our God. They shall still bear fruit in old age; they shall be fresh and flourishing" (Ps. 92:13–14). We never lose our purpose when we are motivated by love.

The Dearly Departed

Romans 7:7–12

7 What shall we say then? Is the law sin? Certainly not! On the contrary, I would not have known sin except through the

law. For I would not have known covetousness unless the law had said, "You shall not covet."

8 But sin, taking opportunity by the commandment, produced in me all manner of evil desire. For apart from the law sin was dead.

9 I was alive once without the law, but when the commandment came, sin revived and I died.

10 And the commandment, which was to bring life, I found to bring death.

11 For sin, taking occasion by the commandment, deceived me, and by it killed me.

12 Therefore the law is holy, and the commandment holy and just and good.

In a news conference several years ago, cable TV mogul Ted Turner declared that the Ten Commandments were obsolete. Appearing before the National Newspaper Association in Atlanta, Turner said that the biblical Ten Commandments do not relate to current global problems such as overpopulation and the arms race.

The apostle Paul could not disagree more. In Romans 7:7 he asks, **Is the law sin?** His response is an emphatic **Certainly not!** Even though we are no longer bound to the Law, it still serves a purpose:

a. *The Law serves as a reminder of sin* (vv. 7–9). The law is not sin; it is neutral. But it reminds us what is sin. The posted speed limit on most U.S. interstate highways is 65 miles an hour. Suppose you were late for an engagement, chose to drive 75 miles per hour and were pulled over by a state trooper. You could not say, "That speed sign back there made me do it." You made the choice to go 75. All the speed sign did was inform you what would constitute sin. If it had not been there, you could have claimed ignorance. But because the sign was there and you knew the law but chose to break it, you are guilty of sin. Don't try to divert the blame.

b. *The Law serves as a reminder of our powerlessness* (vv. 10–11). The Law informs us that sin kills. Paul says, **For sin, taking occasion by the commandment, deceived me, and by it killed me** (v. 11). The Law cannot protect; it can only predict. Satan is a deceiver. He tells us that we can get around God's commandments and do what we want. The Law says we cannot. I once heard Vance Havner say, "You can't break the law of God; you break yourself against the law of God. If you jump off a tall building, you don't break the law of gravity. You break your head, but not the law of gravity." In our helplessness, the Law points us toward the Savior but it cannot save us. It is as helpless as we are.

c. *The Law serves as a reminder of God's holiness* (v. 12). The Commandments and Law are a reflection of God's holiness. They remind us of the perfection necessary to be acceptable to God. No sin can come into the presence of God. A certain soap product is advertised as being "99.44% pure." That may be quite an accomplishment for soap, but it would be blasphemous as a statement about God. God is infinitely perfect in His holiness. Not the slightest degree of sin taints His character. His holiness is reflected in the Law.

The Struggle Goes On

Romans 7:13–25

13 Has then what is good become death to me? Certainly not! But sin, that it might appear sin, was producing death in me through what is good, so that sin through the commandment might become exceedingly sinful.

14 For we know that the law is spiritual, but I am carnal, sold under sin.

15 For what I am doing, I do not understand. For what I will to do, that I do not practice; but what I hate, that I do.

16 If, then, I do what I will not to do, I agree with the law that it is good.

17 But now, it is no longer I who do it, but sin that dwells in me.

18 For I know that in me (that is, in my flesh) nothing good dwells; for to will is present with me, but how to perform what is good I do not find.

19 For the good that I will to do, I do not do; but the evil I will not to do, that I practice.

20 Now if I do what I will not to do, it is no longer I who do it, but sin that dwells in me.

21 I find then a law, that evil is present with me, the one who wills to do good.

22 For I delight in the law of God according to the inward man.

23 But I see another law in my members, warring against the law of my mind, and bringing me into captivity to the law of sin which is in my members.

24 O wretched man that I am! Who will deliver me from this body of death?

25 I thank God—through Jesus Christ our Lord! So then, with the mind I myself serve the law of God, but with the flesh the law of sin.

Some people assume that the longer you travel, the easier it gets. It is true that as you travel you pick up hints and tips that can ease your journey, but to say it ever gets easy is a gross exaggeration. In fact, in the physical world, many people change jobs simply because they cannot stand traveling any more.

The spiritual world has it parallels. Paul describes these struggles as:

a. *Current* (v. 14–24). Paul couches these verses in the present tense. The experiences he describes not only occurred when Paul first became a Christian, but they were an ongoing struggle even though he was spiritually mature. Some Christians harbor the fallacy that there will come a day when spiritual struggles will be behind them. They hope some experience or act of discipline will put them beyond the reach of temptation. But this is wishful thinking. Until we reach heaven, there will always be a struggle.

b. *Carnal* (v. 14). Paul says, **I am carnal.**[1] This does not mean that

---

[1] The Greek word is *sarkinos*. According to Trench (*Synonyms of the New Testament*, p. 254), the ending –*inos* designates "the stuff of which anything is made." Often it is used to designate attitudes or behavior contrary to righteous living, but it also can mean "physical flesh" as opposed to spiritual. Paul uses it in this latter sense.

Paul was habitually sinning. Rather, he is saying that he lived in a body of flesh and blood. As a consequence, the sensual nature of the world still appealed to him. No matter how hard we try to suppress it, the biological composition of our body will be attracted to the things of the world. Therefore, Satan will never cease using sensual allurements to gain a foothold in our lives.

c. *Spiritual* (v. 14). Behind the physical struggle is a spiritual struggle. Paul says, "For we do not wrestle against flesh and blood, but against principalities, against powers, against the rulers of the darkness of this age, against spiritual hosts of wickedness in the heavenly places" (Eph. 6:12). We cannot expect to win our battle with the flesh using fleshly weapons. We can isolate ourselves on some deserted island, lock ourselves away in a monastery or seclude ourselves in some secret place, but Satan will still find us—and find a way to get a toehold in our lives.

There is an old story about the devil crossing the Libyan desert. He came upon a number of his little fiends tormenting a holy hermit. The sainted man easily shook off all their evil suggestions. The devil watched their failure and then stepped forward to give them a lesson. "What you do is too crude," he said. "Permit me but a moment." With that he whispered to the holy man, "Your brother has just been made bishop of Alexandria." A scowl of malignant jealousy quickly clouded the hermit's serene face. "That's more what I had in mind," the devil said.

It is impossible to hide from Satan or avoid temptation. Therefore, we must learn to use spiritual weapons (see Eph. 6:11–18). Unless we know how to do spiritual battle, we will never see victory.

d. *Hopeful* (v. 25). After the anguished cry of verse 24, Paul turns to the one Person who gives hope—the Lord Jesus Christ. As challenging as your struggle may be, there is always hope in Christ. In Him the victory is won. You may lose some battles along the way, but Christ has won the war. A day is coming when the struggle will be over. Until that day, however, fight on. The hymn writer says, "Lead on, O King Eternal, Till sin's fierce war shall cease, and holiness shall whisper the sweet Amen of peace."

CHAPTER 8

Freeway Ahead
Romans 8:1–39

Those who travel by car know the joy of seeing the sign "Freeway Ahead." After driving for hours on a torturous two-lane highway, stopping at every intersection and slowing down for every small town, they soon will be cruising down a multilane thoroughfare with no impediments and no oncoming traffic. What a contrast! What freedom!

Romans 8 has that same feeling. After reading the wretched cry of a doomed man in Romans 7:24, how wonderful it is to read in Romans 8:1, **There is therefore now no condemnation.** We turn from condemnation to celebration, from the helplessness of the Law to the victory of the cross.

Signposts Aloft

Romans 8:1

1 There is therefore now no condemnation to those who are in Christ Jesus, who do not walk according to the flesh, but according to the Spirit.

As we travel we encounter many signs put up for our benefit. Most are ordinary cautions, such as "Curve Ahead" or "Deer Crossing." Occasionally, however, we will come across a sign that demands our immediate attention, such as "Dead End" or "Bridge Out." In these situations we must respond immediately.

Romans 8:1 is one of those spiritual signs that needs our immediate attention. It is not only thought-provoking, it is life-changing. It has numerous implications:

a. *It implies we are part of God's family* (Rom. 8:15). We have gone from the dungeons to the dining room, from "aliens and strangers" to God's own beloved children. We have an eternal home. A coworker of mine adopted two Korean children. The judge who ratified the adoption told him, "You realize that once this procedure is over, there is no turning back. There are no second thoughts. They are your children forever." When we are adopted into God's family, there is no turning back. God will never have second thoughts. We are His forever.

b. *It implies we are a new person* (2 Cor. 5:17). God is not in the remodeling business. He does not simply want to make us better people but different people. Man is good at cobbling—he adds a little here and mends a little there. God wants to start new from the foundation up. The Christian faith is not a self-improvement project but a self-replacement project.

c. *It implies that we are a piece of God's work* (Eph. 2:10). We are God's workmanship. God is at work making a masterpiece that will be so wondrous we can scarcely imagine it. Our part in this great undertaking is to be patient and cooperate. Michelangelo painted the Sistine Chapel, on and off, for 37 years. Had someone decided to hurry him along by helping him, his work would have been ruined. Often we try to help God by grabbing the brushes and adding our own childish drawings. Let us take our hands off and let the Master work. He who began a good work in you will finish it (Phil. 1:6).

d. *It implies that we are saints* (Rom. 1:7; 1 Cor. 1:2; 2 Cor. 1:1) Every Christian is a saint even if he does not always act that way. The word translated "saint" literally means "holy one" or "set apart one." We are set apart to serve God. During the reign of Oliver Cromwell, the British government began to run low on silver for coins. Lord Cromwell sent his men to search the local cathedral to see if they could find any precious metal there. After investigating, they reported, "The only silver we could find is in the statues of the saints standing in the corners." To which the radical soldier and statesman of England replied, "Good! We'll melt down the saints and put them into circulation!" Our function is not to decorate church corners but to occupy street corners, not to seclude ourselves from the world but to be the salt and light of the world.

New Vistas

Romans 8:2-11

2 For the law of the Spirit of life in Christ Jesus has made me free from the law of sin and death.

3 For what the law could not do in that it was weak through the flesh, God did by sending His own Son in the likeness of sinful flesh, on account of sin: He condemned sin in the flesh,

4 that the righteous requirement of the law might be fulfilled in us who do not walk according to the flesh but according to the Spirit.

5 For those who live according to the flesh set their minds on the things of the flesh, but those who live according to the Spirit, the things of the Spirit.

6 For to be carnally minded is death, but to be spiritually minded is life and peace.

7 Because the carnal mind is enmity against God; for it is not subject to the law of God, nor indeed can be.

8 So then, those who are in the flesh cannot please God.

9 But you are not in the flesh but in the Spirit, if indeed the Spirit of God dwells in you. Now if anyone does not have the Spirit of Christ, he is not His.

10 And if Christ is in you, the body is dead because of sin, but the Spirit is life because of righteousness.

11 But if the Spirit of Him who raised Jesus from the dead dwells in you, He who raised Christ from the dead will also give life to your mortal bodies through His Spirit who dwells in you.

One of the exciting results of traveling is seeing new scenery—to view snowcapped mountains, to gaze upon a billowing ocean or to stand beneath giant sequoia trees. As we discover one magnificent vista after another, we begin to realize that we worship an awesome Creator.

But God is equally impressive when we consider our lives in Christ.

As we make our way through the journey into life, we find that there are all sorts of new "scenery":

a. *We have a new position: free* (vv. 2–4). During a visit to the United States, Alexander Solzhenitzn told of an experience that occurred when he was in a labor camp in the Soviet Union. Because of physical and emotional abuse, he became so discouraged that he considered suicide. One day he was given a rest break, and a man he had never met nor saw again sat down beside him. Without saying a word, the stranger picked up a stick and drew a cross on the ground. Solzhenitzn said that as he sat there and stared at the cross the truth suddenly dawned on him. "I realized therein lies man's freedom." Even though he was a prisoner in a labor camp, he had more freedom because of Christ than his guards did. Freedom is a matter of the spirit, not the body. When we accept Christ, we are freed from the burden of guilt and the fear of death. The price is paid and the bondage is gone.

b. *We have a new mind: heavenly* (vv. 5–7). Minds have to be occupied by something—they are not meant to be empty. If a person's primary interest is this earthly life, his mind will be filled with earthly (fleshly) concerns. Since earthly things are only temporary, he lives in fear of losing them. He is caught up in striving to get more while protecting what he has. He has no peace or joy. On the other hand, the one who has his heart set on heaven has a mind filled with spiritual affairs. These are eternal and safely protected. Therefore, he has a peace that the earthly minded will never know.

c. *We have a new fellowship: pleasing* (vv. 8–9). The basis for pleasing God, as we have seen elsewhere, is faith (Heb. 11:6). The Holy Spirit is the One who creates that faith in us. He generates the faith to believe and sustains that faith as He indwells us. This makes our lives pleasing to God. No matter how noble and good a life an unbeliever may seek to live, without a Spirit-induced faith he cannot please God.

d. *We have a new hope: the resurrection* (vv. 10-11). The basis for hopelessness and despair is death because all things end in the grave. But for a Christian this is not true.

In Catherine Marshall's book *A Man Called Peter*, she tells the story of a young, terminally ill son asking his mother what death was like, if it hurt. "Kenneth," she said, "you remember when you were a tiny boy how you used to play so hard all day that when night came you would be too tired even to undress, and you would tumble into mother's bed and fall asleep? That was not your bed—it was not where you belonged. And you would only stay there a little while. In the morning, much to your surprise, you would wake up and find yourself in your own bed in your own room. You were there because someone had loved you and taken care of you. Your father had come—with big, strong arms—and carried you away.

"Kenneth, death is just like that. We just wake up some morning to find ourselves in the other room—our own room where we belong—because the Lord Jesus loved us." He never questioned again. And several weeks later he fell asleep just as she had said.

But the outlook gets even better. Because for Christians, **Christ will also give life to [our] mortal bodies.** The bodies we leave behind when we go to be with Jesus will be resurrected, glorified and restored to us. We know that this is true because **the Spirit of Him who raised Jesus from the dead dwells in you.**

Sonship

Romans 8:12–17

12 Therefore, brethren, we are debtors—not to the flesh, to live according to the flesh.

13 For if you live according to the flesh you will die; but if by the Spirit you put to death the deeds of the body, you will live.

14 For as many as are led by the Spirit of God, these are sons of God.

15 For you did not receive the spirit of bondage again to fear, but you received the Spirit of adoption by whom we cry out, "Abba, Father."

16 The Spirit Himself bears witness with our spirit that we are children of God,

17 and if children, then heirs—heirs of God and joint heirs

with Christ, if indeed we suffer with Him, that we may also be glorified together.

In early Colonial days, some people were so desirous of coming to this new land that they sold themselves as indentured servants. In return for passage to America, they consented to serve for an agreed-upon amount of time in the home of their benefactor.

In our journey into life, however, we do not travel as servants but as sons. Paul says, **For as many as are led by the Spirit of God, these are sons of God.** A son has a totally different relationship with the master of the house than a servant. A son's relationship is

a. *Intimate* (v. 15). Paul says, **We cry out Abba**. The word *Abba* is the term that a small child would call his father. It means "daddy." No servant would dare to address the head of the home in such a way. Only a dearly loved child would use such a word. As God's children, it is our privilege to approach God the Father as our daddy. This does not mean we can show Him any less respect, but it is the respect shown to a trusted father rather than a dreaded master.

b. *Assured* (v. 16). Children who are abandoned by their father never know for sure who he might be. Some have testified that when they encounter age-appropriate men, they wonder, *Could this be my father?* There is no such doubt for a child of God. The Holy Spirit bears witness that **we are children of God**. We have the assurance that we belong.

c. *Glorious* (v. 17). The future for a child of God just keeps getting better and better. Paul says that someday we will be **heirs of God and joint heirs with Christ.** In 1960 John F. Kennedy was seeking the Democratic nomination for president. While campaigning, he visited a coal mine in West Virginia. During a question-and-answer period following his speech, one of the miners asked him, "Is it true you're the son of one of our wealthiest men?" Kennedy had to admit it was true. "Is it true that you've never wanted for anything and had everything you wanted?" Again Kennedy had to agree. "Is it true you've never done a day's work with your hands all your life?" A bit embarrassed, Kennedy nodded that this was true. Then the miner said, "Let me tell you something. You haven't missed a thing." What Kennedy possessed was his by inheritance, not by his efforts. He was an heir to a wealthy father—and so are Christians.

Road Hazards I

Romans 8:18–23

18 For I consider that the sufferings of this present time are not worthy to be compared with the glory which shall be revealed in us.

19 For the earnest expectation of the creation eagerly waits for the revealing of the sons of God.

20 For the creation was subjected to futility, not willingly, but because of Him who subjected it in hope;

21 because the creation itself also will be delivered from the bondage of corruption into the glorious liberty of the children of God.

22 For we know that the whole creation groans and labors with birth pangs together until now.

23 And not only they, but we also who have the firstfruits of the Spirit, even we ourselves groan within ourselves, eagerly waiting for the adoption, the redemption of our body.

A road hazard may range all the way from broken glass strewn on the highway to a blizzard. Those in the transportation industry know the significance of road hazards, so they have produced road hazard tires, road hazard insurance, etc. The goal is to assist the traveler through these hazards as best as possible.

A spiritual journey has its share of hazards as well. In the first centuries of the church, the hazards included having one's possessions confiscated—or even death. In most places today the hazards are not quite that severe, but they still exist. Paul offers some important reminders for those encountering the hazards of the journey:

a. *These afflictions are light* (v. 18). *Light* and *heavy* are comparative terms. A book is heavy compared to a feather. A book is light compared to a steel anvil. Our trials sometimes seem heavy—even more than what we think we can bear. But Paul says when we experience the glory of heaven, our tribulations will seem insignificant. There is such a vast contrast that our current difficulties are **not worthy to be compared with**

the glory which shall be revealed in us. Always weigh today's experiences by tomorrow's promises.

b. *These afflictions are common* (vv. 19–21). When experiencing the hazards of life, it is common to think that we are all alone, that we are the only ones going through difficult times. That is not true. Paul says that **creation itself** needs to be delivered from the **bondage of corruption** (v. 21). When Adam and Eve disobeyed, the consequences fell on every living thing. Death, pain and chaos became a part of life. If you asked 20 people if they are having difficult problems *right now*, 10 would probably say yes. This means we can find a lot of comfort and understanding from our brothers and sisters in Christ. They have been (or are) in our situation and can provide the support through Christ to see us through.

c. *These afflictions are temporary* (vv. 22–23). Paul calls these hardships "birth pangs." Birth pangs, fortunately, do not go on forever. They only exist until the baby is born. That does not mean they are not painful. Most mothers say that birth pangs are the most severe pain they have ever endured. But the joy of holding a newborn child makes them seem insignificant. When we experience afflictions, we must remember that these, too, are a sign of something greater yet to come. When that greater comes, the trials will cease.

Road Hazards II

Romans 8:24-28

24 For we were saved in this hope, but hope that is seen is not hope; for why does one still hope for what he sees?

25 But if we hope for what we do not see, we eagerly wait for it with perseverance.

26 Likewise the Spirit also helps in our weaknesses. For we do not know what we should pray for as we ought, but the Spirit Himself makes intercession for us with groanings which cannot be uttered.

27 Now He who searches the hearts knows what the mind of the Spirit is, because He makes intercession for the saints according to the will of God.

28 And we know that all things work together for good to those who love God, to those who are the called according to His purpose.

Reminders are great. Without watch alarms or those little reminders that pop up on our computer screens, some of us would be late for everything. Reminders prepare us ahead of time so we are not caught by surprise when the hazards of life jump out in front of us. But what can we do? How can we actively change our situation? Paul says

a. *Do not give up* (v. 25). One of the important keys in our spiritual journey is to not give up. There will be days of discouragement and defeat. In *Remember All the Way*, William Townsend, founder of Wycliffe Missions, tells of an evangelist who was so discouraged he planned to quit. He told a friend, "Don Guillermo, I'm going to quit." Guillermo replied, "Why do you give your resignation to me? When you began your service, you said the Lord Jesus Christ was calling you to tell others about Him. I think you'd better present your resignation to the One who called you. Let's get down on our knees here, and you tell Him that you are going to quit. Let Him hear what you've just told me—that it's too hard, that too many people criticize you. Tell the Lord—He's the One who sent you."

"Well, I hesitate to do that," the evangelist replied. "I'm afraid He'll tell me to stay with the job." "If that's what He wants, don't you think you'd better stay?" "Yes, I think I should!" the evangelist responded. Taking new strength and refusing to look back, the man went on to faithfully serve the Lord.

Unless the Lord says otherwise, never give up. As Samuel Chadwick advised, "If you're successful, don't crow. If you fail, don't croak.

b. *Pray in the Spirit* (vv. 26-27). This does not mean praying in an unknown tongue; it means praying in submission to the Holy Spirit. The Holy Spirit always knows the perfect will of God. Therefore, we must be willing to let the Spirit pray through us what is God's will even if it is not our will.

At the funeral of a beloved pastor, the speaker said to the congregation, "I know you prayed for your pastor, and some of you may be in danger of concluding that God did not hear your prayers. He does indeed hear prayer. But in this situation two prayers may have been

101

prayed. You may have prayed, 'O God, spare his life, for we need him so badly.' The Spirit's groaning prayer may have been, 'Take him away, for the congregation is learning too heavily on him, not upon Thee.'" God then answered the prayer that the Spirit prayed on their behalf. To truly pray in the Spirit is to submit to His will.

c. *Move forward confidently* (vv. 28). Fear paralyzes us. It keeps us from doing what we need to do. But fear dissipates when we realize that God has everything under control. For the child of God, He truly does work **all thing together for good**. That does not mean that all things *are* good. But like a weaver, God blends the dark strands in with the light to make a perfect picture. In fact, without the dark strands the picture would be like an overexposed photo—washed out and unattractive. We can move forward confidently, knowing that God will use all of our experiences to create His perfect will for our lives.

The Longest Trip

Romans 8:29–30

29 For whom He foreknew, He also predestined to be conformed to the image of His Son, that He might be the firstborn among many brethren.

30 Moreover whom He predestined, these He also called; whom He called, these He also justified; and whom He justified, these He also glorified.

A trip up the Nile River, the world's longest river, is a journey of 3,470 miles. If you chose to take a trip around the world (and stayed strictly on the equator), you would transverse 24,901.55 miles. Either of these would be a long trip, but the longest of all is encompassed in Romans 8:29–30. These verses describe a trip that begins in eternity past and ends in eternity future. This trip has five ports of call:

a. *Foreknowledge* (v. 29). The word *foreknowledge* simply means "to know beforehand." It is true that foreknowledge means that God knows in advance the events that will happen, but that by itself is an oversimplification. If God simply looked down into history and saw what we were going to do, and then as a result of that knowledge predestined us to do it, it would not make Him much of a sovereign God. That would make the creature sovereign over the Creator. Instead, to foreknow means to "know with paternal love" (cf. Amos 3:2;1 Cor. 8:3).

b. *Predestination* (v. 29). The word *predestination* sometimes causes horror in the minds of people. But it should not; it is a biblical word that means to "predetermine," "to decree from eternity past." Yet we must never equate this doctrine with fatalism. Fatalism says that the world is plunging headlong toward an indeterminate end. Nobody knows what will happen—it just will happen. Paul, however, teaches that there is a definite and determinate end for those who are "the called." God has predestined us to an end, and that is to be conformed to the image of His Son. No matter what Satan throws at us, we will someday be like Jesus.

c. *Calling* (v. 30). As believers, we were foreknown in eternity past and were foreordained prior to our birth. Yet in the present time God does not manipulate us like puppets. He calls us. He owes us. He beseeches us. He asks us to receive His offer of salvation. The word *called* means "to give a name to" or "to call out of." Right now God's work in salvation is calling. He wants to name you as His.

d. *Justification* (v. 30). There is no calling without justifying. This means God treats us and declares us to be righteous. We have a right relationship with Him. That does not mean our behavior is always righteous, but God treats us as if we were righteous.

e. *Glorification* (v. 30). This is yet to happen. Although the process of glorification begins in the present, it will reach its completion either when we die or when Christ returns again. Still, every day as we open His Word and study about Him we reflect a little more of the image of Christ. But the day is coming when we will take a quantum leap and perfectly reflect the character of God's Son. Then we will be truly glorified.

More Than Conquerors

Romans 8:31–39

31 What then shall we say to these things? If God is for us, who can be against us?

32 He who did not spare His own Son, but delivered Him up for us all, how shall He not with Him also freely give us all things?

33 Who shall bring a charge against God's elect? It is God who justifies.

34 Who is he who condemns? It is Christ who died, and furthermore is also risen, who is even at the right hand of God, who also makes intercession for us.

35 Who shall separate us from the love of Christ? Shall tribulation, or distress, or persecution, or famine, or nakedness, or peril, or sword?

36 As it is written: "For Your sake we are killed all day long; We are accounted as sheep for the slaughter."

37 Yet in all these things we are more than conquerors through Him who loved us.

38 For I am persuaded that neither death nor life, nor angels nor principalities nor powers, nor things present nor things to come,

39 nor height nor depth, nor any other created thing, shall be able to separate us from the love of God which is in Christ Jesus our Lord.

Sir Edmund Hillary, who attempted to scale Mount Everest, lost one of the members of his team in the failed effort. He returned to a hero's welcome in London, England, where a banquet held in his honor was attended by the lords and ladies and powerful people of the British Empire. Behind the speakers' platform were blown-up photographs of Mount Everest. When Hillary arose to receive the acclaim of the distinguished audience, he turned around and faced the mountain and said, "Mount Everest, you have defeated me. But I will return. And I will defeat you. Because you can't get any bigger and I can."

We all suffer defeat sometimes in our journey into life. Satan presents an especially alluring bait, or we become careless, or we choose to be disobedient; the trap snaps and down we go. But it is not the end. It does not destroy our salvation. In fact, Paul gives us four assurances concerning our salvation:

a. *It is safe from the hands of men* (v. 31). No man gave us our salvation, and no man can take it away. A new Christian gave his testimony in his church. With a smile on his face and great joy in his heart, he told how God had delivered him from a life of sin. The person in charge of the service was legalistic and did not appreciate the reality of salvation by grace alone, so he said to the young man, "You seem to indicate that God did everything when He saved you. Tell us about your part in coming to Christ." The man quickly answered, "Oh, I did my part all right. For more than thirty years I ran away from God as fast as I could. That was my part. But God took after me and ran me down. That was His part." No one can overwhelm your salvation or take it away from you, because God has done His part.

b. *It is safe from being inadequate* (v. 32). In ancient times whole cities were abandoned because of an inadequate supply of food or water. In our own time, inadequate supplies of vital resources, such as oil, have caused crises around the world. But God is always adequate. And if He has not denied us even His own Son, He will not deny us anything else. We will lack nothing that we need for our faith or life. We therefore have to assume if there is something missing in our life, we actually do not need it.

c. *It is safe from accusations* (v. 33). Who can say anything against you that will take away your salvation? Who can bring a charge against you and say, "By the way, do you know what this person did after he was saved?" Only the One who justified us can, and He has promised, "I will never leave you nor forsake you" (Heb. 13:5). Anybody can make a charge, but only God can make a Christian. If you have trusted Jesus as your Savior, rejoice in the fact that nobody can drag anything out of your past or present that would cause you to lose what God has done in your life.

d. *It is safe from spiritual powers* (v. 38). Satan's goal is to destroy mankind, and he will use all the minions of hell if he must to do so. This goes especially for the Christian. But Paul assures us that Satan will fail. He may go about like a roaring lion, seeking whom he may devour, but God has put him on a chain. Satan can bring temptation and trials into our lives, but he is not allowed to do us any real harm. We are as safe from him as a child in his mother's arms, because God loves us. Satan can do nothing to change that.

CHAPTER 9

The Scenic Route
Romans 9:1–33

Sometimes when whizzing down the interstate you are offered the opportunity to exit onto an older, two–lane highway that was built years earlier (when getting to your destination in the shortest time possible was not the top priority). This allows you to take in the scenery. Certainly, these scenic routes are slower, but the countryside and panoramas can be breathtaking. Hurried travelers rarely avail themselves of these opportunities and consequently miss the best part of the trip.

Paul offers the "scenic route" through chapters 9–11. After reading Romans 8, it would be possible to skip chapters 9–11, begin reading again at Romans 12, and everything would still fit neatly together. The logic of Paul's argument would be uninterrupted. But you would miss one of the best parts of the trip. All of Romans deals with God's righteousness. In chapters 9–11 Paul shows that God is righteous in His choices— specifically, His choice of Israel as the people of God.

Telling People the Hard Truth

Romans 9:1–3

1 I tell the truth in Christ, I am not lying, my conscience also bearing me witness in the Holy Spirit,

2 that I have great sorrow and continual grief in my heart.

3 For I could wish that I myself were accursed from Christ for my brethren, my kinsmen according to the flesh,

Occasionally we must tell someone something he would rather not hear. We try to be delicate, but it does not always work. For example, an elderly countess was very happy with her chauffeur. He was courteous, prompt and efficient. The only complaint she had concerned his personal appearance. One day she said to him diplomatically, "Randall, how frequently do you think one should shave in order to look neat and proper?" Also trying to be diplomatic, Randall said, "Well, madam, with a light beard like yours, I'd say every three or four days would be enough."

Paul had to tell the truth to his kinsmen. They had rejected the Messiah and failed God. He knew the subtle approach would not work, so he chose a more direct confrontation. Still, he did it in such a way as to minimize the offense. Telling people the hard truth works best if done

a. *Sincerely* (v. 1). Paul says, **I tell the truth in Christ, I am not lying, my conscience also bearing me witness in the Holy Spirit**. Antisthenes the Cynic Philosopher said, "There are only two people who will tell you the truth about yourself—an enemy who has lost his temper and a friend who loves you dearly." Those who need to hear the hard truth must be convinced that we are telling them the truth because we are sincerely concerned for them (Prov. 27:5–6). The truth teller must not hide any ulterior motives.

b. *Sorrowfully* (v. 2). Hard truths are seldom joyful. The situation with his kinsmen caused Paul **great sorrow and continual grief**. Even though many of his countrymen harassed Paul and sought to prevent the spread of the Gospel, he was saddened by their plight rather than bitter. You are not ready to share a hard truth until your heart is broken by it.

c. *Sacrificially* (v. 3). Paul was so deeply concerned about the salvation of the Jews he says, **For I could wish that I myself were accursed from Christ for my brethren, my kinsmen according to the flesh.** Of course, Paul could not actually take Israel's sin upon himself. He knew that. Christ had already died to atone for those sins. Israel only had to accept Jesus' completed work on the cross. Yet Paul says, "If I could, I would be willing to be **accursed**."[1] People are more open to

---

[1] Gk: *anathema* literally means "under the ban." When a heathen city was taken in Old Testament times, it was sometimes put "under the ban." That meant everything in the city was utterly destroyed.

listening to hard truths if they know you will stick by them sacrificially. They want the assurance that instead of standing on the bank and throwing stones, you are willing to get in the canoe and help paddle.

Everything to Gain

Romans 9:4–8

4 who are Israelites, to whom pertain the adoption, the glory, the covenants, the giving of the law, the service of God, and the promises;

5 of whom are the fathers and from whom, according to the flesh, Christ came, who is over all, the eternally blessed God. Amen.

6 But it is not that the word of God has taken no effect. For they are not all Israel who are of Israel,

7 nor are they all children because they are the seed of Abraham; but, "In Isaac your seed shall be called."

8 That is, those who are the children of the flesh, these are not the children of God; but the children of the promise are counted as the seed.

So many people who have it all still manage to mess up their lives. Suicides among the rich and famous are far more common than among those who have much less.

The Israelites had been given so much in their spiritual lives, yet they failed to reach the goals God desired for them. Paul implies at least three reasons for Israel's failure:

a. *They rested on their privileges* (v. 4). What privileges did the Israelites enjoy? They were set apart by God from the rest of the nations (**adoption**). He blessed them with His presence (**the glory**), with His **covenants** and His **Law**. God gave them the opportunity to serve Him and promised many more blessings if they would be faithful. But what did they do with all these blessings? They enjoyed them, but they did not share them. The Israelites were content as long as they had a relationship with God. They did not care if anyone else did.

Christians are also a privileged people. We have the Bible, the Holy Spirit and the Church. Most of all we have the answer to man's greatest problem—sin. But besides enjoying them, what do we do with these blessings? Like the Israelites, we are content to rest on our privileges rather than share them. We need to heed the warning of Archie Parish: "A person who is content to go to heaven alone probably isn't going there at all."

b. *They rejected their Savior* (vv. 5-6). In addition to many privileges, Israelites also had great honor. Their history is replete with such famous **fathers** as Abraham, Moses, David, Solomon and Elijah, to name a few. The greatest honor was also theirs: they were chosen as the channel through which the **Christit**[2] would come. Yet when He came, the apostle John tells us, "His own did not receive Him" (John 1:11). They were looking for a conquering hero, not an itinerant preacher. They were expecting Him to be rich and powerful, not a poor carpenter. They rejected the only Messiah they will ever have!

We experience Christ's presence with us in many ways—some of them far different from what we expect. In speaking of the poor, the imprisoned, the helpless, Jesus said, "Assuredly, I say to you, inasmuch as you did it to one of the least of these My brethren, you did it to Me" (Matt. 25:40). A nineteenth century painting shows a long row of beggars waiting in a soup line. They are all ragged and dirty. But around the head of one is a barely perceptible halo. One of them is Christ! You may not see a halo around the heads of those in need, yet to serve them is to serve Christ. If we should turn them away, we may be turning away our Savior.

c. *They relied on the externals* (vv. 7–8). They were confident that because they were Jews they would automatically go to heaven. Many people are like that. They are depending on their parents' faith or that they have been baptized or gone through some religious instruction. Others expect living a "good life" will open the doors of heaven. But Paul says that it is **the children of the promise** (who) **are counted as the seed**. Only those who accept the promise of salvation in Jesus Christ shall be saved.

---

[2] The Greek translation of the Hebrew word for *Messiah* ("the anointed one") was "Christ." Since Paul was writing to a primarily Gentile church in Rome, he uses the Greek name rather than the Hebrew.

Who's in Charge?

Romans 9:9–18

9 For this is the word of promise: "At this time I will come and Sarah shall have a son."

10 And not only this, but when Rebecca also had conceived by one man, even by our father Isaac

11 (for the children not yet being born, nor having done any good or evil, that the purpose of God according to election might stand, not of works but of Him who calls),

12 it was said to her, "The older shall serve the younger."

13 As it is written, "Jacob I have loved, but Esau I have hated."

14 What shall we say then? Is there unrighteousness with God? Certainly not!

15 For He says to Moses, "I will have mercy on whomever I will have mercy, and I will have compassion on whomever I will have compassion."

16 So then it is not of him who wills, nor of him who runs, but of God who shows mercy.

17 For the Scripture says to Pharaoh, "Even for this same purpose I have raised you up, that I might show My power in you, and that My name may be declared in all the earth."

18 Therefore He has mercy on whom He wills, and whom He wills He hardens.

Webster's Dictionary defines the word *sovereign* as "one that exercises supreme authority within a limited sphere." Earthly sovereigns exercised their authority over vast areas of land and people. Yet Paul sets about to prove that God is sovereign over all spheres:

a. *He is sovereign over nature* (v. 9). God had promised Abraham, **At this time I will come and Sarah shall have a son.** By nature this was an impossibility. Sarah was 90 years old and far beyond her child bearing years. But God is not hindered by such details. The God who made the laws of nature is able to modify them when He chooses.

b. *He is sovereign over people* (vv. 10–13). God exercised His power of choice by giving Sarah a son. He exercised His power of choice again by choosing one child over another. Verse 10 reminds us of the story of Rebecca, who conceived and bore twins. Paul goes on to say that God chose Jacob, the younger, over Esau, the elder, based on His sovereign will **(for the children not yet being born, nor having done any good or evil, that the purpose of God according to election might stand, not of works but of Him who calls). . . . As it is written, "Jacob I have loved, but Esau I have hated."**[3] While Jacob, the younger, was not the natural choice, he was the sovereign choice. Again, the God who made the law of the firstborn is able to modify it when He chooses.

c. *He is sovereign over the nations* (vv. 14–18). Egypt was the most powerful nation in the Middle East at the time of the Exodus. The Egyptians viewed their Pharaoh as a god. Yet Paul quotes Exodus 9:16, where through Moses God says to Pharaoh, **Even for this same purpose I have raised you up, that I might show My power in you, and that my name might be declared in all the earth.** The mighty leader of this great nation was like putty in God's hands. God allowed him to reach the pinnacle of power so that the nations might marvel even more when God triumphed over him.

God usually operates within a set of laws or principles established by Himself, but these do not limit His sovereignty. The sovereign God is able to do whatever He is moved to do.

It Isn't Fair

Romans 9:19–29

19 **You will say to me then, "Why does He still find fault? For who has resisted His will?"**

20 **But indeed, O man, who are you to reply against God? Will the thing formed say to him who formed it, "Why have you made me like this?"**

---

[3] Hated in the sense of "loved less." By His sovereign right, God chose to exalt Jacob over Esau.

21 Does not the potter have power over the clay, from the same lump to make one vessel for honor and another for dishonor?

22 What if God, wanting to show His wrath and to make His power known, endured with much longsuffering the vessels of wrath prepared for destruction,

23 and that He might make known the riches of His glory on the vessels of mercy, which He had prepared beforehand for glory,

24 even us whom He called, not of the Jews only, but also of the Gentiles?

25 As He says also in Hosea: "I will call them My people, who were not My people, And her beloved, who was not beloved."

26 "And it shall come to pass in the place where it was said to them, 'You are not My people,' There they shall be called sons of the living God."

27 Isaiah also cries out concerning Israel: "Though the number of the children of Israel be as the sand of the sea, The remnant will be saved.

28 For He will finish the work and cut it short in righteousness, Because the LORD will make a short work upon the earth."

29 And as Isaiah said before: "Unless the LORD of Sabaoth had left us a seed, We would have become like Sodom, And we would have been made like Gomorrah."

"It isn't fair!" Every parent has heard these words a thousand times. "It isn't fair! Sally got a bigger ice cream cone than I did." "It isn't fair! Joey got to ride in the front seat last time." "It isn't fair! Jill gets to stay up later than I do." Paul expected some of his readers to have the same reaction. "It isn't fair! How can God hold me responsible when He's the one in control?"

Paul gives a threefold response to this objection:

a. *God has a prerogative to exercise* (vv. 20–21). Paul's reply, **But indeed, O man, who are you to reply against God?**, takes us to the most basic reason: God can do anything He wants. It's similar to a parent's response, "Because I say so." God is not answerable to us, and it is the height of arrogance for the created to question the Creator's motives. We must remember, however, that God's sovereignty will never enable Him to do anything that His moral holiness will not permit Him to do. One divine attribute does not cancel out another.

b. *God has a purpose to accomplish* (vv. 22–24). Paul could have left off his argument here, but he went on. While we may not understand entirely His reasons, we know that God is orchestrating all of history **to show His wrath** (against sin) **and make His power known . . . and that He might make known the riches of His glory on the vessels of mercy, which He had prepared beforehand for glory**. We do not know how everything will work out for our good and God's glory. But it really isn't necessary. Some reporters asked Mrs. Einstein if she understood her husband's theory of relativity. "No," she replied, "but that's OK because I trust my husband." When we do not understand God's purpose, we still must trust His character.

c. *God has a promise to keep* (vv. 25–29). Promises are of great concern in the business community. Writing in the business newsletter *Boardroom Reports*, Robert Half said, "Treat all promises to employees—whether they are expressed or implied—as though they were legal contracts. . . . Write them down and put them in a special file." God treats His promises as special too. No matter how many years go by, God will never forget nor fail to fulfill what He has promised. God made some of these promises through such prophets as Hosea and Isaiah, and He will keep them.

The Fork in the Road

Romans 9:30–33

30 What shall we say then? That Gentiles, who did not pursue righteousness, have attained to righteousness, even the righteousness of faith;

31 but Israel, pursuing the law of righteousness, has not attained to the law of righteousness.

32 Why? Because they did not seek it by faith, but as it

were, by the works of the law. For they stumbled at that stumbling stone.

33 As it is written: "Behold, I lay in Zion a stumbling stone and rock of offense, And whoever believes on Him will not be put to shame."

In the children's fantasy *Alice in Wonderland*, Alice came to a fork in the road that led in different directions. She asked the Cheshire Cat for advice. "Cheshire-Puss—would you tell me please, which way I ought to go from here?" "That depends a good deal on where you want to get to," said the Cat. "I don't much care where," said Alice. "Then it doesn't matter which way you go," said the Cat.

Unfortunately, the clever feline was wrong when it comes to real life. Each choice (even the small ones) makes a difference. C. S. Lewis wrote, "Every time you make a choice you are turning the central part of you . . . into something a little different than it was before. And taking your life as a whole, with all your innumerable choices, you are slowly turning this central thing either into a Heavenly creature or into a hellish creature."[4] Making the wrong choice in a children's story may lead only to adventure, but in real life it can lead to disaster.

Israel and the Gentiles traveled together for much of the Book of Romans. They both stood guilty and condemned before the throne of God. They both were offered salvation through Jesus Christ. At this fork in the road they chose to go separate ways. Paul explains the choices each one of us must make when confronted with the Gospel:

a. *We must choose between self and God* (vv. 30–31) At the root of all Israel's problems (and ours) was pride. They did not want to be in God's debt. They pursued the Law zealously to make themselves worthy of God; but their focal point was still on themselves. They believed they had it within themselves to be the righteous people God required them to be. Unlike the Gentiles, who knew God's righteousness was beyond them, the Jews believed they could achieve it if they only tried hard enough.

It humbles us to admit something is beyond our ability to

---

[4] C.S. Lewis, *Mere Christianity*, (New York: The Macmillian Company, 1952), p. 92.

accomplish. We want to believe that if we live better, work harder, give more, we might possibly be able to reach our goal. But God says, "Give it up!" We have to give up on ourselves and choose God if want to have His righteousness. The focus is on God, not self.

b. *We must choose between Law and grace* (v. 32). The Jews found grace to be a stumbling block. Peter said, "Therefore, to you who believe, He is precious; but to those who are disobedient, 'The stone which the builders rejected has become the chief cornerstone,' and 'A stone of stumbling And a rock of offense.'' They stumble, being disobedient to the word, to which they also were appointed" (1 Pet. 2:7–8).

The Law is so logical—do this and you will live. Grace says, "Die and you will live." This goes against what we think makes sense. The Law commands; grace entreats. This is contrary to our concept of authority. The Law costs—blood, sweat and tears. Grace is free. This does not fit our understanding of justice. Those determined to make their own way will find grace offensive. It goes against everything they view as right. For many people it is still a cause for stumbling.

c. *We must choose between works and faith* (v. 33). Works are more appealing to the unbeliever than faith. Works are measurable. They can be seen, touched, counted and praised. Faith, on the other hand, appears as this nebulous something that has to be taken, well, on faith.

Thus the choice comes between something we can see, touch and feel and something that we simply have to trust. The latter is more difficult, but it is necessary. Christ is no longer bodily in our midst. The work of the cross is not accessible to our five senses. But the work accomplished there by Christ makes our righteousness possible. As tempting as it is to look to the physical for our salvation, we must choose faith instead.

Once you read this chapter in Romans you may feel that your are a born loser. You don't stand a chance of eternal salvation. But you are not a born loser; you are a born chooser. Just make sure you make the right choice. Choose the Law and lose; choose the Lord Jesus and win.

CHAPTER 10

A Heart's Desire
Romans 10:1–21

On August 3, 1492, Christopher Columbus set sail on a journey that took him into uncharted seas. During the arduous journey his crew and he encountered storms, damage to their ships and shortages of food and water. Still they pressed on. Columbus was determined to realize his heart's desire—to find a shorter trade route to Asia. Although he failed to reach this goal, the intrepid mariner achieved something even greater. On October 12, 1492, he landed at Guanahani, an island in the Bahamas. This began the exploration of the new world.

Romans 10 reveals that Paul had a heart's desire too. Despite the fact that he was the apostle to the Gentiles, Paul never lost fervor for his own people. More than anything else, he wanted the Jewish people to experience the same journey into life that he had.

Sincerely Wrong

Romans 10:1–5

1 Brethren, my heart's desire and prayer to God for Israel is that they may be saved.

2 For I bear them witness that they have a zeal for God, but not according to knowledge.

3 For they being ignorant of God's righteousness, and seeking to establish their own righteousness, have not submitted to the righteousness of God.

4 For Christ is the end of the law for righteousness to everyone who believes.

5 For Moses writes about the righteousness which is of the law, "The man who does those things shall live by them."

When the Crystal Palace Exhibition opened in 1851, people flocked to London's Hyde Park to marvel at the technology. One of the newest technologies at the time was the use of steam power. On display were steam plows, steam locomotives, steam looms, steam organs and even a steam cannon.

But the first-prize winner that year was a steam invention with 7,000 parts. When it was turned on, its pulleys, whistles, bells and gears made a lot of noise, but the machine did not do anything! It was simply 7,000 moving parts making a lot of commotion.

The Jews of Paul's day also made a lot of commotion. In fact, the Romans regarded them as a contentious people. But they were going nowhere. Their journey was not taking them closer to God. They were zealous (even Paul admits that), but:

a. *Being zealous is no substitute for being correct* (v. 2). Paul said **they have a zeal for God, but not according to knowledge**. Zeal is a commendable attribute. In fact, many Christians who hold the right doctrines could use a good deal more zeal. Oliver Wendell Holmes said, "I might have entered the ministry if certain clergymen I knew had not looked and acted so much like undertakers." Robert Louis Stevenson once wrote in his diary, "I have been to church today, and am not depressed." It must have been an unusual experience for him.

The zealousness of some cults puts many real Christians to shame. Most churches could use a few more "amens" and "hallelujahs." But enthusiasm must never become a substitute for correct doctrine. Much preaching today could use a little more heat, but it must be preaching that also generates light. Heat and light should not be separated. Let's make sure our doctrine conforms to the Scriptures—and then go full speed ahead.

b. *Being zealous is no substitute for being righteous* (vv. 3–4). The Jews were convinced that no one could be as enthusiastic and dedicated to God as they were. This belief soon degenerated into a subtle self-righteousness. Their zeal itself became the way to God rather than an expression of their relationship with God. Righteousness (a right relationship with God) is a gift. It is received, not earned. First we must get our relationship with God right, and then He will bless our zeal to do good deeds.

c. *Being zealous is no substitute for being perfect* (v. 5). The religious leaders of Paul's time thought of themselves as good people. Many of them were. They were moral, conscientious, religious individuals. But they were imperfect. They would not think of committing adultery, but Jesus said, "Whoever looks at a woman to lust for her has already committed adultery with her in his heart" (Matt. 5:28). They tithed even the herbs from their garden—mint, anise and cummin—but they failed to fulfill the weightier matters of the law—justice, mercy and faith. Jesus did not condemn them for tending to these small details but said, "These you ought to have done, without leaving the others undone" (Matt. 23:23).

It is good to be zealous, but to get to heaven you have to be perfect. Even one failure destroys any hope of getting into God's kingdom. Paul quotes Moses, who said, **The man who does those things shall live by them**. James says, "For whoever shall keep the whole law, and yet stumble in one point, he is guilty of all" (James 2:10). Therefore, it is not sufficient to keep the law zealously; you must keep it perfectly.

The Essential

Romans 10:6–13

6 But the righteousness of faith speaks in this way, "Do not say in your heart, 'Who will ascend into heaven?'" (that is, to bring Christ down from above)

7 or, "'Who will descend into the abyss?'" (that is, to bring Christ up from the dead).

8 But what does it say? "The word is near you, even in your mouth and in your heart" (that is, the word of faith which we preach):

9 that if you confess with your mouth the Lord Jesus and believe in your heart that God has raised Him from the dead, you will be saved.

10 For with the heart one believes to righteousness, and with the mouth confession is made to salvation.

11 For the Scripture says, "Whoever believes on Him will not be put to shame."

12 For there is no distinction between Jew and Greek, for the same Lord over all is rich to all who call upon Him.

13 For "whoever calls upon the name of the LORD shall be saved."

Some things are important—others are essential. I have learned through years of traveling to foreign countries to make sure I have what I need before I leave home. Nothing is more frustrating than to arrive at my destination and discover that I have left ties, a toothbrush or my travel alarm at home. Are these really essentials? Maybe not. I can purchase another tie. Some hotels provide a toothbrush in the room. And I can always request a wake–up call for the morning. But there is one essential I can't replace overseas—my passport.

As Paul discusses the subject of righteousness, he says there are many things that are important, but one only is essential for having a right relationship with God. That is faith in the finished work of Jesus Christ on our behalf at Calvary. Such faith is

a. *Always available* (vv. 6–8). No great feats are necessary to trust Christ. Paul says, **But the righteousness of faith speaks in this way, "Do not say in your heart, 'Who will ascend into heaven?'"** (that is, to bring Christ down from above) or, **"'Who will descend into the abyss?'"** (that is, to bring Christ up from the dead). We do not have to perform impossible tasks or have mystical experiences to have faith in Christ. Saving faith is always accessible to us because it is the gift of God (Eph. 2:8) and He is always accessible to us. We learn how to appropriate God's gift of faith from reading His Word. Paul says, **The word is near you, even in your mouth and in your heart.** The Jews constantly discussed the salvation God planned for Israel. But even though God's Word was frequently in their mouths and even in their hearts, it was all itellectual. They lacked God's one essential—faith. Faith was available, but it was never appropriated.

b. *Always rational* (v. 9). Someone once defined faith as "believing in something with no evidence." That's not biblical faith, the kind of faith that leads to salvation. The Christian faith is based on a body of solid evidence, at the center of which is the resurrection of Christ. Paul says you must **confess with your mouth the Lord Jesus and believe in your heart that God has raised Him from the dead**. This kind of faith is "substantial" faith; it has a basis and leads to a journey into life.

In the early part of the twentieth century, a group of lawyers met in England to explore the biblical accounts of Jesus' resurrection. They wanted to see if the case as stated in Scripture would hold up in a court of law. When their study was finished, they concluded that Christ's resurrection was one of the best-established facts of history! You do not have to leap into the dark in order to have faith in Jesus Christ. Faith is not a leap but a gift, God's gift.

c. *Always confessional* (vv. 10–11). The only requirement for our salvation is faith in Christ. We are never permitted to add to this requirement. However, the kind of faith that leads to salvation also leads to confession. It is life–changing faith, leading us from the moment of salvation to a journey into life everlasting. With salvational faith there is a subsequent change in our behavior, so that **with the heart one believes to righteousness and with the mouth confession is made to salvation**. Genuine faith that brings righteousness to the heart will not fail to bring confession to the lips. We may not all express our faith the same way, but true faith, salvational faith, is confessional faith. It's hard to keep quiet about good news.

d. *Always sufficient* (v. 13). Notice that the verse does not say, "hope to be saved," or, "might be saved." Instead it says, **shall be saved**. This is a promise. Some people may be concerned about their past sins, sins that are reprehensible to our society. But faith in Jesus Christ is sufficient for forgiveness. Others may be living lifestyles that are immoral and destructive. But faith in Jesus Christ is sufficient for deliverance. Still others worry about their future. What if they surrender their lives to Christ and then are tempted to go back into sin? Faith in Jesus Christ is sufficient for victory. Whatever the time, whatever the need, faith in Jesus Christ is always enough.

Getting the Job Done

Romans 10:14–21

14 How then shall they call on Him in whom they have not believed? And how shall they believe in Him of whom they have not heard? And how shall they hear without a preacher?

15 And how shall they preach unless they are sent? As it is written: "How beautiful are the feet of those who preach the gospel of peace, Who bring glad tidings of good things!"

16 But they have not all obeyed the gospel. For Isaiah says, "Lord, who has believed our report?"

17 So then faith comes by hearing, and hearing by the word of God.

18 But I say, have they not heard? Yes indeed: "Their sound has gone out to all the earth, And their words to the ends of the world."

19 But I say, did Israel not know? First Moses says: "I will provoke you to jealousy by those who are not a nation, I will anger you by a foolish nation."

20 But Isaiah is very bold and says: "I was found by those who did not seek Me; I was made manifest to those who did not ask for Me."

21 But to Israel he says: "All day long I have stretched out My hands To a disobedient and contrary people."

When faced with making a journey, the first things you must ask are, What is it going to take to get me there? Can I drive? Do I need to take a plane? How much money must I spend on transportation? How many travel days am I willing to endure? Setting out on a journey always involves a great deal of planning to get the job done.

In the previous verses Paul spoke about the need for righteousness. The approach the Jews were taking was not going to make it (vv. 1–5). Then he offered God's solution—Jesus Christ (vv. 6–13). The need was present—a lack of righteousness; the solution was present—Jesus Christ.

But how could the two get together? Paul says it takes three elements to get the job done:

a. *It takes a messenger* (vv. 14–15). The questions in these verses are asked regressively: How shall they call on Him in whom they have not believed? How can they believe in Him of whom they have not heard? How shall they hear without a preacher? And finally, how shall those who have that responsibility fulfill it unless they are sent? Paul wants to focus on the sending of the preacher. Everything builds to that moment of truth—how will he get there unless he is sent?

God could have arranged for the Gospel to be shared in many ways. He could have written it in the skies. He could have sent out angels. Instead, He chose to spread the truth through human beings.

It is said that after Christ returned to heaven He was approached by an angel. The angel asked, "What did you do on earth to insure that the Gospel would be preached after you left?" "I left twelve men to share the Good News," Christ replied. "But what if they fail," the angel asked, "what other plan do you have?" "There is no other plan," Christ responded.

Calling a person to the work of the ministry is God's responsibility. Sending that person to where the Gospel needs to be preached is our responsibility. *Tie in mission statistic 5.3 billion people 1.3 saved*

b. *It takes the Word* (vv. 16–18). Scripture is the only instrument God has promised to use to engender faith. A person can share his opinions, insights and thoughts with others, but without the assurance of "Thus saith the Lord," it will be to no avail. Faith comes by hearing, but not hearing just anything. It must be the **word of God**. When the Word is faithfully preached, it will not come back empty-handed.

c. *It takes an obedient heart* (vv. 19–21). A messenger and a message are necessary, but so is an obedient heart. Isaiah speaks for God when he says, **All day long I have stretched out My hands to a disobedient and contrary people**. God can save anyone except those who refuse to be saved. No sin is so big that it can block the highway to heaven. No problem is so insurmountable that it cannot be overcome in Christ. But our attitude can bring all these other efforts to nothing. Recently, a news magazine reported that 50 percent of employers claim that attitude is the major problem with new employees.[1] Sometimes in order to get the job done an attitude adjustment is necessary.

Getting God's salvation and man's need together is not difficult for those who see themselves as part of God's solution. If God has called you to be His messenger and has given you His message, be obedient. Obedience is the key to getting the job done.

---

[1] David P. Jones, "Did you know that . . . ," *Bottom Line*, August 15, 1995, p. 15.

CHAPTER 11

The Remnant
Romans 11:1–36

In the first several waves of migration to the American West, many families started out on the journey, but only a remnant made it to the West Coast. Some turned back, others settled along the way, and many lost their lives. Only the hardiest and most determined got all the way to the Pacific Ocean. This small remnant became the population base for California, Oregon and Washington.

God also has a remnant. In His faithfulness through the centuries, He has maintained a minority who has endured hardship and persecution yet survived to proclaim the true Gospel. Despite the rejection of the many, God always keeps a few who are committed to Him. This is true of the nation of Israel today. There is a remnant of believing Jews (Messianic Jews), proving God is not yet finished with His people.

Never Abandoned

Romans 11:1–10

1 I say then, has God cast away His people? Certainly not! For I also am an Israelite, of the seed of Abraham, of the tribe of Benjamin.

2 God has not cast away His people whom He foreknew. Or do you not know what the Scripture says of Elijah, how he pleads with God against Israel, saying,

3 "LORD, they have killed Your prophets and torn down Your altars, and I alone am left, and they seek my life"?

4 But what does the divine response say to him? "I have

reserved for Myself seven thousand men who have not bowed the knee to Baal."

5 Even so then, at this present time there is a remnant according to the election of grace.

6 And if by grace, then it is no longer of works; otherwise grace is no longer grace. But if it is of works, it is no longer grace; otherwise work is no longer work.

7 What then? Israel has not obtained what it seeks; but the elect have obtained it, and the rest were hardened.

8 Just as it is written: "God has given them a spirit of stupor, Eyes that they should not see And ears that they should not hear, To this very day."

9 And David says: "Let their table become a snare and a trap, A stumbling block and a recompense to them;

10 Let their eyes be darkened, that they may not see, And bow down their back always."

The book *The Day America Told the Truth* reported a survey of adults who were asked, "What would you be willing to do for ten million dollars?" One out of four said they would abandon their entire family for ten million dollars. Twenty–three percent said they would become prostitutes for a week. Three percent said they would put their children up for adoption, while others said they would leave their husband or wife.

Fortunately, God is not so fickle. He never abandons His people. The Jews are God's "peculiar" people (Titus 2:14; 1 Pet. 2:9, KJV), meaning His own people. In spite of their rebellion and waywardness, God has maintained a remnant of Jews for Himself. Paul offers three reasons why:

a. *Because of God's faithfulness* (vv. 1–4). Paul uses himself as an example. He was as much a Jew as it was possible to be: **of the seed of Abraham, of the tribe of Benjamin**. Paul had even persecuted the church (Acts 8:3). Yet God remained faithful to him and at the appropriate time appeared to him and called him to preach the Gospel he had tried to destroy. Having personally experienced God's faithfulness, Paul says, **God has not cast away His people whom He foreknew**. The fact that God not only knew beforehand, but from the foundation of the world set His love upon His people, makes it impossible for Him to retract that love.

English hymn writer William Cowper was a Christian but often sank into despair. One foggy night he called for a horse–drawn carriage to take him to the London Bridge, where he intended to commit suicide by jumping in the Thames River. But after two hours of driving through the mist, the coachman reluctantly confessed that he was lost. Disgusted by the delay, Cowper left the carriage and decided to find the bridge on foot. After walking only a short distance, he discovered he was at his own doorstep! Immediately he recognized the restraining hand of God. Convicted by the Spirit, he realized that the way out of his troubles was to trust the faithfulness of God, not to jump into the river.

God will be faithful even when we are unfaithful. When God loves a nation or an individual, He never gives up. Like the hound of heaven, He pursues him until His will is done.

b. *Because of God's grace* (vv. 5–6). The basis for this remnant is **according to the election of grace**. Nothing about Israel merited the favor God showed toward them. They were disobedient and stiffnecked. Elijah says of them, **LORD, they have killed Your prophets and torn down Your altars** (v. 3). Grace, however, is not based on who we are or what we do but on God's love for us.

During the Spanish-American War, Clara Barton, the founder of the Red Cross, was working in Cuba. One day Colonel Theodore Roosevelt came to her and offered to buy food for some of his sick and wounded Rough Riders. She refused to sell it to him. Roosevelt could not understand. He cared about his men enough to pay for the supplies out of his own pocket. When he complained to the surgeon in charge, he said, "Colonel, just ask for it!" A smile broke over Roosevelt's face. Now he understood—the provisions were not for sale. When he simply asked, he got the food at once. In the same way, grace is something God gives, not something we can buy or earn. All we must do is ask.

c. *Because of God's sovereignty* (vv. 7–10). Scripture records that to the majority of Israelites, **God has given . . . a spirit of stupor, Eyes that they should not see And ears that they should not hear, to this very day** (cf. Deut. 29:4; Isa. 29:10). Some people might object, "That is not fair!" Yet it is fair because God is sovereign. Paul then quotes from Psalm 69:22–23, where David writes of his fellow Jews who would reject and crucify the Messiah: **Let their table become a snare and a trap, A stumbling block and a recompense to them; Let their eyes be darkened, that they may not see, And bow down their back always.** Like Elijah, David would have condemned them all, yet God does not. He chooses some and gives the rest what they want—a hardened heart.

A man came to his pastor and said, "Pastor, I have problems with the first chapter of Malachi, where it says, 'Jacob I have loved, but Esau I have hated.'" "Yes," the minister said, "that's a difficult verse, but which part troubles you?" "The latter part, of course," the man answered. "I cannot understand why God should hate Esau." The pastor replied, "That verse has often bothered me as well, but my difficulty has always been with the first part. I never could understand why God loved that rascal Jacob."

God in His sovereignty has chosen some on whom He wishes to bestow favor. We may wonder about it, but we cannot object. It is God's sovereign right, and whatever the holy God does must be imminently just and fair, as well as sovereign.

More to Come

Romans 11:11–15

11 I say then, have they stumbled that they should fall? Certainly not! But through their fall, to provoke them to jealousy, salvation has come to the Gentiles.

12 Now if their fall is riches for the world, and their failure riches for the Gentiles, how much more their fullness!

13 For I speak to you Gentiles; inasmuch as I am an apostle to the Gentiles, I magnify my ministry,

14 if by any means I may provoke to jealousy those who are my flesh and save some of them.

15 For if their being cast away is the reconciling of the world, what will their acceptance be but life from the dead?

Several decades ago, the Burma Shave company hit on a unique advertising scheme. It posted a series of signs along major highways with the words of a jingle, such as "Feel your face / as you drive by / Don't you think / you should try / Burma Shave." Each sign contained just enough of the jingle to keep you looking forward to the next one. When you sighted the first one, you knew there was more to come.

For the Jewish nation there is also "more to come." Paul asks, **I say then, have they stumbled that they should fall?** That is, "Has God eternally rejected them?" He answers his own question vigorously, **Certainly not!** God has at least three reasons for allowing the Jewish nation to stumble:

a. *To enrich the world* (v. 12). The apostle John wrote, "For God so loved the *world* that He gave His only begotten Son, that whoever believes in Him should not perish but have everlasting life" (John 3:16, italics mine). God carries the whole world in His heart. Whether they accept Christ or not, He cares about them. Furthermore, God's gift of His Son demonstrates to them His love and concern. We can never allow ourselves to be any more narrow in our love than God is. If God loved the world, we must love the world also.

b. *To enrich the Gentiles* (v. 12). More specifically, God brought the wealth of justification to the non–Jewish portion of the world. God meant for the Israelites to be His witness to the pagan nations around them. They failed. God has now transferred that responsibility to the Church, which today is made up primarily of Gentiles. In the process God has bestowed upon the Church inestimable riches—the Holy Spirit, spiritual gifts, the fruit of a noble character, power over the forces of darkness, eternal life, etc. The Gentiles have been made wealthy with treasures that no amount of money could buy.

c. *To provoke the Jews* (vv. 11, 14). Twice in this passage Paul mentions that God wants to use the Gentiles to cause the Jews to desire a saving relationship through Jesus. In fact, God wants to make them jealous. No emotion energizes people like jealousy. Shakespeare called it a "green–eyed monster." But handled appropriately, jealousy can cause people to do what they ought to do. As the Jews see their God at work in the Gentile nations, one day they will want the same experience. Their jealousy will drive them to where God has always wanted them to be—in a personal relationship with Him.

A Lesson in Horticulture

Romans 11:16–24

16 For if the firstfruit is holy, the lump is also holy; and if the root is holy, so are the branches.

17 And if some of the branches were broken off, and you, being a wild olive tree, were grafted in among them, and with them became a partaker of the root and fatness of the olive tree,

18 do not boast against the branches. But if you do boast, remember that you do not support the root, but the root supports you.

19 You will say then, "Branches were broken off that I might be grafted in."

20 Well said. Because of unbelief they were broken off, and you stand by faith. Do not be haughty, but fear.

21 For if God did not spare the natural branches, He may not spare you either.

22 Therefore consider the goodness and severity of God: on those who fell, severity; but toward you, goodness, if you continue in His goodness. Otherwise you also will be cut off.

23 And they also, if they do not continue in unbelief, will be grafted in, for God is able to graft them in again.

24 For if you were cut out of the olive tree which is wild by nature, and were grafted contrary to nature into a cultivated olive tree, how much more will these, who are natural branches, be grafted into their own olive tree?

Travel gives us the opportunity to learn firsthand about other countries. If you were to travel through Israel, you would discover that growing olives is still an important business. The wood is used for everything from construction to woodcarving. The fruit is exported all around the world.

You would also learn that there is a wild olive tree and a cultivated olive tree. Each has its strengths and weaknesses. The wild olive has a sturdy root system, but its branches do not bear quality fruit. The cultivated olive tree has quality fruit but a poor root system. The solution? Graft the stem of a young cultivated olive tree onto the root system of a wild olive tree. When it grows up, it will have the best of both worlds.

Paul uses this same analogy to describe what God has done with the Gentile believers, only "contrary to nature" (v. 24). In other words, God has turned the process around and grafted wild olive branches (the Gentiles) onto the roots of cultivated trees (Israel). In light of this, Paul reminds the Gentiles of three important truths:

a. *Gentiles are outsiders* (vv. 16–17). Originally, all of us who are Gentiles were "aliens from the commonwealth of Israel and strangers from the covenants of promise, having no hope and without God in the world" (Eph. 2:12). It is only by God's grace that we were chosen to be grafted into the root when the original branches were broken off. As we enjoy life in Jesus Christ and all the good things that come from our journey into life, let us remember who we are. We are holy because **the root is holy** (v. 16). We can take no credit for the blessings we have.

b. *Gentiles draw strength from the root* (v. 18). Jews have been discriminated against by Gentiles (even Christian Gentiles) for centuries. They have been called "Christ killers" and driven from one country to another. Many forget what a tremendous debt we owe these people. It is their history, their legacy, even their ancestry that provides the basis for our beliefs. How anemic our faith would be without Abraham, Moses, Samuel, David, Isaiah and many more. In fact, if it were not for the Jews, we would not even have a Savior. Jesus was a Jew. Even though they have failed in many ways, God has still used the Jewish people to bless us immensely.

c. *Gentiles are expendable* (vv. 19–24). The people of Israel lost their blessings because of unbelief. Yet **if God did not spare the natural branches, He may not spare you either.** We need to take care that we do not think that God cannot do without us. If we choose not to believe, God will deal with us in the same fashion. We are only a blip in God's dealing with the nation of Israel. As God's primary concern was the Jewish nation in the Old Testament, so Israel will be His primary concern in the future. The church age is like a parenthesis within a sentence. It momentarily interrupts the flow of words, but then it ends and the sentence continues. We are living in a parenthesis today, but the rest of the sentence is coming.

A Divine Mystery

Romans 11:25–32

25 For I do not desire, brethren, that you should be ignorant of this mystery, lest you should be wise in your own opinion, that hardening in part has happened to Israel until the fullness of the Gentiles has come in.

26 And so all Israel will be saved, as it is written: "The Deliverer will come out of Zion, And He will turn away ungodliness from Jacob;

27 For this is My covenant with them, When I take away their sins."

28 Concerning the gospel they are enemies for your sake, but concerning the election they are beloved for the sake of the fathers.

29 For the gifts and the calling of God are irrevocable.

30 For as you were once disobedient to God, yet have now obtained mercy through their disobedience,

31 even so these also have now been disobedient, that through the mercy shown you they also may obtain mercy.

32 For God has committed them all to disobedience, that He might have mercy on all.

In modern terms a mystery is a puzzle or riddle that has not yet been solved. In biblical terms, however, a mystery is a secret that has been or is being disclosed. Not every detail may be known, but the general outline of what has or will transpire is shared. Thus, Paul calls Israel's fall and restoration a "mystery." It is beyond our total understanding, but we do know that

a. *Israel's rejection is temporary* (v. 25). Israel has been removed from center stage only **until the fullness of the Gentiles has come in**. Until God is finished dealing specifically with the Gentiles in salvation, you can anticipate that Jewish people will not come to the Lord Jesus in great numbers. However, when the complete number of Gentiles is saved, spiritual blindness will fall from the eyes of God's people, and great revivals will break out among the Jews.

b. *Israel's salvation will be total* (vv. 26–28). This does not mean every individual Jew will one day be saved. God always saves on the basis of faith, not nationality, and faith is an individual matter. Numerous interpretations of this phrase have been offered. John Calvin suggested that "all Israel"[1] referred to the total number of the elect throughout all history, both Jew and Gentile. A more likely conclusion is that Paul is talking about the remnant living on the earth at Christ's return. These shall "all be saved." Regardless of how "all Israel" is to be interpreted, Paul says that the nation of Israel will turn en masse to their Messiah when He returns. What a glorious day that will be.

c. *Israel's future is assured* (vv. 29–32). Verse 29 proclaims, **For the gifts and the calling of God are irrevocable**. God will not go back on His promises. God is not finished with His people. As a nation, Israel's future is sealed. One day Jesus will come out of Zion as the Deliverer. When that happens, all those who have not believed God in the past will obtain mercy, and, if they place their faith in Jesus Christ, they, too, will be saved.

When All Is Said and Done

Romans 11:33–36
33 **Oh, the depth of the riches both of the wisdom and**

---

[1] The Greek word for *all* is *pas*. The early Jews understood this to mean the nation Israel. In the Mishnah of the Sanhedrin it says, "All Israel has a portion in the age to come." But then it goes on and names Israelites who will not have a portion in the age to come. It is evident that they believed God would deal with the nation, but not every individual within the nation.

knowledge of God! How unsearchable are His judgments and His ways past finding out!

34 "For who has known the mind of the LORD? Or who has become His counselor?"

35 "Or who has first given to Him And it shall be repaid to him?"

36 For of Him and through Him and to Him are all things, to whom be glory forever. Amen.

Paul finishes chapters 9 through 11 with a doxology. There are times when we handle mysteries so staggering that our theology turns to hymnology and we can only sing God's praise. We are at one of those times.

As we consider the temporary rejection of the Jews, the gracious election of the Gentiles and the future hope of Israel, our minds are easily overwhelmed. We have to agree with the apostle Paul that all of this is

a. *Unfathomable* (vv. 33–34). Parts of the ocean floor cannot be reached by human divers or even robotic probes. They are unfathomable. Yet the wisdom and knowledge of God are even more unreachable. In Isaiah we read, "For My thoughts are not your thoughts, nor are your ways My ways," says the LORD. "For as the heavens are higher than the earth, so are My ways higher than your ways, and My thoughts than your thoughts" (Isa. 55:8–9). Even if God were to reveal His mysteries to us, they would be deeper than we could comprehend.

b. *Uncontrollable* (v. 35). One way humans have of controlling others is to get them into their debt. It may be a moral obligation (I did this favor for you, now you owe one to me) or an actual debt (Proverbs 22:7 tells us we become a servant to the one we borrow from). But God is no man's debtor. No one can say to Him, "You must do this because You owe me something." What God does, He does of His own free will, not because He is obligated.

c. *Indisputable* (v. 36). When we realize the greatness of God, there is only one appropriate response—surrender. The word *amen* means "so be it." We are beyond the point of trying to understand; we no longer seek explanations but recognize that God is not within our control, so we give in. So be it. Whatever God wants, let it be. We will deny Him nothing.

CHAPTER 12

The Sacrificed Life
Romans 12:1–21

Every journey involves sacrifice. Traveling is never as comfortable as being at home. Travel requires that you sit for hours in cramped seats on a plane, ride for days in a hot car, sleep in unfamiliar beds and eat fast food that all begins to taste the same. But when you arrive, the sacrifices are usually worth it all.

The journey into life is the same. It's not all fluffy pillows and soft recliners. God's people must make sacrifices along the way. The apostle Paul gives us some insight into these sacrifices.

The Essential Sacrifice

Romans 12:1

¹ I beseech you therefore, brethren, by the mercies of God, that you present your bodies a living sacrifice, holy, acceptable to God, which is your reasonable service.

Have you ever watched a pigeon and wondered why it walks so funny? Scientists say that a pigeon's peculiar gait allows it to see where it is going. A pigeon cannot adjust its focus while on the move, so between steps it comes to a complete stop, refocuses on the ground and then takes the next step.

Christians find it beneficial to stop once in a while and refocus as well, especially when we consider the matter of sacrifice. What kind of a sacrifice are we supposed to make?

a. *A living sacrifice* (v. 1). Some Christians die in sacrifice to their Lord. More Christians have been murdered for their faith in the twentieth century than in all others centuries combined. According to Christian Solidarity International, more than 150,000 Christians are martyred every year.[1] While most believers are not martyred for their faith, all Christians are called to be living sacrifices. Paul entreats us, in light of God's mercies, that we offer our bodies as a living sacrifice. This may be the hardest sacrifice of all. Someone said, "The problem with a living sacrifice is that it keeps crawling off the altar." But living sacrifices speak softly and tenderly of God's grace and mercy.

Adoniram Judson, missionary to Burma, endured tremendous hardships while trying to reach the unsaved for Christ. He spent 17 months in Ava Prison, where he was terribly mistreated. For the rest of his life he carried the scars made by the chains and iron shackles used to bind him. Upon his release he courageously asked for permission to go to another province to preach the Gospel. The ruler of Burma denied his request, saying, "My people are not fools enough to listen to anything a missionary might say, but I fear they might be impressed by your scars and turn to your religion."

God is not so much interested in our dying for our faith as He is in our living for the faith. He is not looking for your sacrifice of death but your sacrifice of life. A living sacrifice can be a dynamic force to draw others to a living Savior.

b. *A holy sacrifice* (v. 1). The word *holy* means to be set apart, to be used exclusively for the purpose of God. "But as He who called you is holy, you also be holy in all your conduct" (1 Pet. 1:15). When a Christian offers his body as a holy sacrifice, he subordinates all his rights to the purpose and plan of God. God has exclusive claim to him, all that he has, all that he is, all that he will be. It is God's choice to allow that sacrificed body to be sick or well, to live or die. It is His to use as He sees fit. The sacrificed life has no temporal guarantees, only the eternal God. And that is enough!

---

[1] "The Persecuted Church," *National & International Religion Report*, February 20, 1995, Vol. 9, No. 5, p. 7.

c. *An acceptable sacrifice* (v. 1). What makes a sacrifice acceptable to God? Genesis records that both Cain and Abel brought a sacrifice to the Lord, but God found Abel's sacrifice acceptable and not Cain's (Gen. 4:3–5). What made the difference? The answer is faith. "By faith Abel offered to God a more excellent sacrifice than Cain, through which he obtained witness that he was righteous" (Heb. 11:4). Our sacrifice is acceptable only as we let go and totally trust God with our lives. In faith we offer Him ourselves and He finds us acceptable.

d. *A reasonable sacrifice* (v. 1). Such a total surrender is not unreasonable when one considers God's sacrifice. He gave His only begotten Son as an offering for our sins. Redeemed people find it logical to reciprocate God's love by living the sacrificed life. Giving ourselves completely to God is not unreasonable because He does not ask from us more than what He gave to us.

A Sacrifice That Isn't

Romans 12:2
2   And do not be conformed to this world, but be transformed by the renewing of your mind, that you may prove what is that good and acceptable and perfect will of God.

David Livingstone recorded in his journal, "People talk of the sacrifice I have made in spending so much of my life in Africa. . . . Away with such a view and with such a thought! It is emphatically no sacrifice. Say rather it is a privilege."

When our life is surrendered to Christ, we become transformed.[2] The Holy Spirit renews our minds, a process not unlike deleting files from a computer and replacing them with new files. The result is that we see sacrifice from an entirely new perspective. Instead of drudgery, God's will appears:

---

[2] The Gk. *metamorphousthai* implies more than an external change. The change begins from the inside and works it way out. From this word we derive our English word *metamorphosis*, which means to change strikingly in appearance and/or character.

a. *Good* (v. 2). Few things are truly good. Usually when we try to do something "good" there are selfish motives involved, even though they may be deeply buried. God's will, however, is always good. He has no ulterior motives to taint His plans. God assures us, "For I know the thoughts that I think toward you, says the LORD, thoughts of peace and not of evil, to give you a future and a hope" (Jer. 29:11).

b. *Acceptable* (v. 2). When we go through difficulties, we are repulsed by the thought that this might be God's will for our life. We cry out, "Why, Lord? Why have You allowed such a thing?" Yet as we mature in Christ, the "why" question is asked less frequently. We develop a steadfast confidence that God's will is best. We learn to accept His will even when we don't understand it.

c. *Perfect* (v. 2). The word *perfect* implies "complete," "with no parts missing." God's will for us does not leave out the tiniest factor. So often some minutia ruins our plans. On January 28, 1986, seven astronauts lost their lives because an O–ring seal on the space shuttle *Challenger* malfunctioned. Small omissions can cause great disasters. But God never leaves out a single detail, no matter how little it might be. His will is always for our good, acceptable and complete.

The Sacrifice of Independence

Romans 12:3–16

3 For I say, through the grace given to me, to everyone who is among you, not to think of himself more highly than he ought to think, but to think soberly, as God has dealt to each one a measure of faith.

4 For as we have many members in one body, but all the members do not have the same function,

5 so we, being many, are one body in Christ, and individually members of one another.

6 Having then gifts differing according to the grace that is given to us, let us use them: if prophecy, let us prophesy in proportion to our faith;

7 or ministry, let us use it in our ministering; he who

teaches, in teaching;

8 he who exhorts, in exhortation; he who gives, with liberality; he who leads, with diligence; he who shows mercy, with cheerfulness.

9 Let love be without hypocrisy. Abhor what is evil. Cling to what is good.

10 Be kindly affectionate to one another with brotherly love, in honor giving preference to one another;

11 not lagging in diligence, fervent in spirit, serving the Lord;

12 rejoicing in hope, patient in tribulation, continuing steadfastly in prayer;

13 distributing to the needs of the saints, given to hospitality.

14 Bless those who persecute you; bless and do not curse.

15 Rejoice with those who rejoice, and weep with those who weep.

16 Be of the same mind toward one another. Do not set your mind on high things, but associate with the humble. Do not be wise in your own opinion.

One of the earliest television shows I remember watching was *The Lone Ranger*. In each episode this cowboy hero, along with his faithful Indian companion, Tonto, would resolve some Wild West crisis. Together they would then ride off into the sunset, leaving the townsfolk wondering, "Who was that masked man?" Apart from his Indian friend, the Lone Ranger had no lifelong friends, no long-term relationships, no meaningful associations. Even his identity was kept secret. He truly was the *lone* ranger.

While this may have worked in the Old West, the lone ranger approach is inappropriate for the Christian faith. God's plan is for us to be a community, a *koinonia* (fellowship), interdependent, not independent. We need each other. Paul says, **So we, being many, are one body in Christ, and individually members of one another** (v. 5). For each part of the body to function together as a single organism rather than a gang of lone rangers, we need to

a. *Think realistically* (v. 3). Nothing throws the body out of balance more quickly than one member with exaggerated self–esteem. A Christian is **not to think more highly than he ought**. The opposite is also true. We are to think **soberly**, or realistically, about ourselves, to make an honest assessment of our strengths and weakness. Then we should find a place in the body where our strengths can be used and our weaknesses shored up.

b. *Contribute spiritually* (vv. 4–8). Every Christian possesses at least one spiritual gift. Paul lists several of them in these verses: prophecy (v. 6), ministry (v. 7), teaching (v. 7), exhortation (v. 8), giving (v. 8), leadership (v. 8) and mercy (8). These gifts are used to build up the body. Each individual contributes his gift to make the body a place where people's needs can be met. The body cannot be at the peak of health unless everyone exercises the gift God has given us.

c. *Love sincerely* (vv. 9–10). Do not fake it! Paul says, **Let love be without hypocrisy.** Zsa Zsa Gabor is famous for calling everyone "darling." She has admitted it is not because she is so fond of people— she just can't remember names. How often do we feign friendship, even Christian love, for someone at church when, in reality, we are harboring bitterness and resentment toward him? Insincere love is worse than indifference; it ultimately causes more hurt.

d. *Grow spiritually* (vv. 11–16). This last group of verses is a potpourri of spiritual advice. If the body of Christ is to function as it ought, Christians must grow up spiritually. The pettiness, vindictiveness and selfishness common in many churches today would disappear if the saints were to commit themselves to spiritual growth. Infancy is the natural consequence of birth, but no one should be stuck in spiritual infancy. "But grow in the grace and knowledge of our Lord and Savior Jesus Christ" (2 Pet. 3:18).

The Sacrifice of Rights

Romans 12:17–21
   17 Repay no one evil for evil. Have regard for good things in the sight of all men.

18 If it is possible, as much as depends on you, live peaceably with all men.

19 Beloved, do not avenge yourselves, but rather give place to wrath; for it is written, "Vengeance is Mine, I will repay," says the Lord.

20 "Therefore if your enemy hungers, feed him; If he thirsts, give him a drink; For in so doing you will heap coals of fire on his head."

21 Do not be overcome by evil, but overcome evil with good.

In Lebanon, New Hampshire, a cook at a Denny's restaurant allegedly spiked two state troopers' eggs with Tabasco sauce. According to friends, he did it because he didn't like policemen. Charges were filed and later dropped, but the man lost his job.

Often we allow our desire for revenge get the better of our good judgment. For an ounce of satisfaction, we receive a pound of trouble. Paul says, **Repay no one evil for evil**. He goes on to tell us why:

a. *As a testimony to others* (v. 17). People watch Christians to see how they act, especially when they confront crisis situations. When wronged, what will a Christian do? To repay good with evil is the mark of Satan. To repay evil with evil is the mark of a man. But to repay evil with good is the mark of God. Which mark will those watching us see?

b. *As an opportunity for God to work* (v. 19). If we fight our own battles, God will not. The night of the Exodus the fleeing Israelites were pursued by the armies of Egypt. After the people crossed the Red Sea, Moses turned to them and said, "Do not be afraid. Stand still, and see the salvation of the LORD, which He will accomplish for you today. For the Egyptians whom you see today, you shall see again no more forever" (Ex. 14:13). After the Israelites crossed the sea on dry ground, God caused the waters to come together again and drown the armies of Egypt. The Israelites did nothing but watch and marvel.

In 2 Chronicles 20, Israel was invaded by the united armies of Moab, Ammon and others. Jehoshaphat appealed to God, who said through the prophet Jahaziel, "You will not need to fight in this battle. Position yourselves, stand still and see the salvation of the LORD" (v. 17). God orchestrated it so that Israel's enemies turned against each other. No one escaped. Instead of having to fight, Judah spent the next three days gathering the spoils.

God does a much better job at exacting justice than we do. It is better to leave the responsibility to Him.

c. *As a means of conquering evil* (v. 20). Darkness cannot be overcome by darkness; you have to turn on the light. When we refuse to treat others as they treat us, we give opportunity for the Holy Spirit to bring conviction upon them.

Richard Weaver was a miner who constantly witnessed to his fellow miners. Most of the men were indifferent, but one became belligerent and finally exclaimed, "I'm sick of your constant preaching. I've a good mind to smack you in the face!" When the man struck him in the face, instead of retaliating, Richard turned the other cheek. Again the man struck him and then walked away, cursing under his breath. Richard called after him, "I forgive you, and pray that the Lord will save you!" The next morning his attacker was waiting for him when he came to work. "Oh, Richard," the man said, his voice filled with emotion, "do you really forgive me for what I did yesterday?" "Certainly," Richard replied, extending his hand. As Weaver told him again the message of salvation, God opened the man's heart, and he received Christ as Savior. Love conquers evil; retaliation only extends it.

d. *As a protection for yourself* (v. 21). The worst evil people can do to you is to get you to hate them. That hatred will do little to harm them, but it will destroy you.

Louis XII understood this principle. Before he became king of France, he was cast into prison by his enemies and kept in chains. Later when he ascended the throne, his advisors urged the king to seek revenge, but he refused. Instead, he prepared a scroll on which he listed all who had committed crimes against him. Beside every man's name he placed a cross in red ink. When his former enemies heard about this, they became frightened and fled. But the king explained, "The cross which I drew beside each name was not a sign of punishment; it was a pledge of forgiveness extended for the sake of the crucified Savior, who upon His cross forgave His enemies and prayed for them."

By extending forgiveness, we keep ourselves from being overcome by bitterness, the most cancerous evil of all.

Living the sacrificed life means submitting our will to the will of God. It means loving without hypocrisy, growing in grace and repaying good for evil. It means reprogramming our minds to have the mind of Christ. We sacrifice all that slows our spiritual growth and gain all that accelerates it. To fail to live the sacrificed life is to fail to allow Christ to live His resurrected life through us (Gal. 2:20). It is to forfeit the blessings of the mercies of God. It's too high a price to pay to get our own way.

CHAPTER 13

Who's in Charge?
Romans 13:1–14

A journey is usually undertaken in the context of authority: airplanes have pilots, ships have captains, trains have engineers. They provide leadership and guidance. Under most circumstances, we court disaster if we choose to disobey these authorities.

In our journey, God also has placed people and principles in authority over us. Paul talks about our relationship to these authorities on our journey into life.

The One Who Bears the Sword

Romans 13:1–7

1 Let every soul be subject to the governing authorities. For there is no authority except from God, and the authorities that exist are appointed by God.

2 Therefore whoever resists the authority resists the ordinance of God, and those who resist will bring judgment on themselves.

3 For rulers are not a terror to good works, but to evil. Do you want to be unafraid of the authority? Do what is good, and you will have praise from the same.

4 For he is God's minister to you for good. But if you do evil, be afraid; for he does not bear the sword in vain; for he is God's minister, an avenger to execute wrath on him who practices evil.

5 **Therefore you must be subject, not only because of wrath but also for conscience' sake.**

6 **For because of this you also pay taxes, for they are God's ministers attending continually to this very thing.**

7 **Render therefore to all their due: taxes to whom taxes are due, customs to whom customs, fear to whom fear, honor to whom honor.**

A little boy wrote to Santa Claus at the North Pole. The letter arrived instead at the office of the Postmaster General, who was touched by its content. The boy did not want toys for Christmas but rather food and clothing for his destitute family. The Postmaster General wrote to the little boy saying that Santa had referred the matter to him and enclosed $50 as a gift from the North Pole. The next year the Postmaster General received another letter addressed to Santa from this boy, which read, "Dear Santa, You were very kind to me last year, and I appreciate it very much. But next time don't send money through the government. You know those guys always keep half of what they get."

The boy's attitude may reflect that of many adults today, but Paul takes the role of government seriously. He says, **Let every soul be subject to the governing authorities** (v. 1). His reasons for yielding to these authorities are significant:

a. *They are ordained of God* (vv. 1–2). Paul lived under a government that was not only secular but idolatrous. The Caesars had appropriated the character of divinity and required their subjects to worship them. Nevertheless, Paul says that **the authorities that exist are appointed by God** (v. 1). For reasons unexplained to us, God allows men, even ungodly men, to come into positions of high authority. God establishes kings and dethrones them (Dan. 4; Prov. 21:1). As a consequence, we need to be cautions when resisting proper authority. Paul even goes so far as to say, **Therefore whoever resists the authority resists the ordinance of God, and those who resist will bring judgment on themselves.** In any situation where the law of the land does not contradict the higher law of Scripture (Acts 5:29), Christians are to obey their leaders despite their personal or political opinions.

b. *They are designed to perpetrate good* (vv. 3–4). Admittedly, government officials do not always appear to make decisions for our good. Governments have conducted ethnic cleansing, unleashed death squads and committed other atrocities. God never condones such behavior. Most governments who do such things, however, do not last long. Justice prevails. No government is perfect, but the majority attempt to keep law and order so that people can live in relative peace and safety. The alternative to government is anarchy, and that never produces desirable results. The period of the judges in Old Testament history proves that (Judg. 21:25). Might becomes right and the law of the jungle prevails. The only thing worse than a bad government is no government.

c. *They are worthy of support* (vv. 5–7). Jesus articulated this principle in Matthew 22:17–21. Approached by the Pharisees about the legality of paying taxes to the brutal and pagan Roman government, Jesus replied, "'Show Me the tax money.' So they brought Him a denarius. And He said to them, 'Whose image and inscription is this?' They said to Him, 'Caesar's.' And He said to them, 'Render therefore to Caesar the things that are Caesar's, and to God the things that are God's.'"

Paul expands on this principle when he says that not only are we to support our government financially (by paying taxes and import/export duties), but also we are to show courtesy (fear) and display esteem (honor) to those who have authority over us. Governments will never be entirely just until the King of Kings sits on the throne of David. Until that day, we are to respect our governments and work to change them when they do not reflect the character of God.

The Debt of Love

Romans 13:8–10

8 Owe no one anything except to love one another, for he who loves another has fulfilled the law.

9 For the commandments, "You shall not commit adultery," "You shall not murder," "You shall not steal," "You shall not bear false witness," "You shall not covet," and if there is any other commandment, are all summed up in this

saying, namely, "You shall love your neighbor as yourself."

10 Love does no harm to a neighbor; therefore love is the fulfillment of the law.

In late 1991, the "on budget" debt for the United States federal government was $3.8 trillion. The "off budget" debt was another $2.5 million. Estimates indicate that by the year 2000 the debt may be as much as $20 trillion. The interest alone on this immense debt would consume all the income taxes paid by Americans.

The frightening prospect that this financial irresponsibility places on future generations of Americans underscores the wisdom of Paul's advice, **Owe no one anything** (v. 8). He does make one exception, however. Verse 8 goes on to say, **except to love one another**. Love is not an option; it is an obligation. Keeping short accounts with others is the purpose behind Paul's financial counsel; keeping long accounts with others is the purpose behind his spiritual counsel. Every traveler on this journey into life is under the authority of love because

a. *Love fulfills the Law* (v. 8, 10). Jesus said, "Do not think that I came to destroy the Law or the Prophets. I did not come to destroy but to fulfill" (Matt. 5:17). Christ's death at Calvary not only gave meaning to the Law and the Prophets, it demonstrated convincingly that God loves people. It was love, not nails, that kept Jesus on the cross. "God demonstrates His own love toward us, in that while we were still sinners, Christ died for us" (Rom. 5:8). In doing that, He fulfilled the Law.

Christ Jesus sacrificed His life for us; Christians are under the same obligation to live the sacrificed life. Obedience done because "the Bible says so" is drudgery; obedience done out of love is a delight. We are constrained not by the letter of the Law but by the spirit of love.

b. *Love sums up the commandments* (v. 9). Some people are proud of the long list of rules they keep. The Pharisees created an organizational system in which they categorized the Mosaic Law into some 365 prohibitions and 250 commandments. Paul says all this is unnecessary if we keep but one commandment: **love your neighbor as yourself**. The purpose of the commandments—You shall not commit adultery; You shall not murder; You shall not steal; You shall not bear false witness; You shall not covet—is to protect our neighbor. **Love does no harm to a neighbor.** If we remember to love our neighbor and look out for his welfare, we have no difficulty in fulfilling the rest of God's law of love. It's the way we live the sacrificed life.

Now More Than Ever

Romans 13:11–14

11 And do this, knowing the time, that now it is high time to awake out of sleep; for now our salvation is nearer than when we first believed.

12 The night is far spent, the day is at hand. Therefore let us cast off the works of darkness, and let us put on the armor of light.

13 Let us walk properly, as in the day, not in revelry and drunkenness, not in lewdness and lust, not in strife and envy.

14 But put on the Lord Jesus Christ, and make no provision for the flesh, to fulfill its lusts.

The more dangerous the conditions, the more important it becomes to have the proper authorities in charge. On March 22, 1994, Russian Aeroflot Flight 593 plunged to the ground, killing all 75 people on board. Investigators discovered that the probable cause of the crash was that the 15–year–old son of Captain Yaroslav Kudrinski was at the controls. Apparently, Captain Kudrinski was teaching his son how to fly the plane when the autopilot disengaged, causing the craft to stall and sending it into a dive. Had the right person been at the controls, the crash may never have happened.

We, too, are headed for dangerous conditions. Paul warns Timothy, "But know this, that in the last days perilous times will come" (2 Tim. 3:1). If Paul could tell the first century Romans, **for now our salvation** (Christ's return) **is nearer than when we first believed** (v. 11), how much more should those words apply to us. As we see the day of our redemption drawing near, we need to pay attention to those authorities who are telling us to:

a. *Wake up* (v. 11). Jesus spent the hours before His arrest praying in the garden of Gethsemane while His disciples slept. They were of no help to Him at all. Many Christians are doing the same today. A sleeping Christian is an unproductive Christian. Souls are not being won for Christ; new believers are not being discipled; God's Word is lying dormant, unread and unheeded. The urgent nature of our day compels Christians to awake and take seriously our responsibilities.

b. *Put on the armor* (v. 12). Paul describes this armor in detail in Ephesians 6:14–17. Each piece is vital to surviving combat: the helmet of salvation, the breastplate of righteousness, the girdle of truth, the shoes of the Gospel, the shield of faith and the sword of the Spirit. Gennady K. Kryuchkov, president of the Council of Evangelical Baptist Churches in Russia, once commented, "In spite of all the complications of our life, path and ministry, if we closely examine our weapons we will find that they are invisible and intangible, and therefore cannot be snatched from us by the KGB or any persecutors in any country. These spiritual weapons . . . cross all borders freely because they are passed vertically, from above. . . . Even though there are so many arrests now, neither prayer nor faith, neither trust nor righteousness have been taken from us. Nothing at all has been taken, because these weapons are made powerful by God!" As the times get more and more dangerous, we will appreciate our armor even greater.

c. *Walk properly* (vv. 13–14). About 900 years ago, Earl Leofric, Lord of Coventry, England, imposed heavy taxes on his people. His wife, Lady Godiva, asked her husband to reduce the revenues. He agreed, but only if she would ride on horseback naked through the town. Though his offer was made sarcastically, she took him up on the deal. The lady asked all the townspeople to stay indoors. Clothed only in her hair, she mounted a horse and rode through the streets. Out of respect for her, all the citizens looked away.

In May 1990, the Board of Aldermen in Winston-Salem, North Carolina, considered a 41 percent hike in property taxes. To protest, an unidentified woman repeated Lady Godiva's act. She rode horseback through the town in nothing but long hair and a flesh-colored body stocking. As she rode through the streets, no one turned away. *Newsweek* reported that men and women "poured into the streets, peered out of windows and climbed to the roofs of buildings to get a good look."

How different and jaded our age is. Society is preoccupied with sex, immodesty and lust. In this darkness, Christians need—now more than ever—to live the sacrificed life, a life of sacrifice to God and those placed in authority by Him. We must set an example for others, not just in what we say but also in what we do. Our walk needs to match our talk. It's the only way to demonstrate in a meaningful way who is in charge.

CHAPTER 14

Journeying Together
Romans 14:1–23

Traveling puts stress on everyone. I read recently of a family who went on vacation. They were 200 miles from home when Dad decided he could not take any more of his two boys bickering in the back seat. "Ever since we left home," he growled, "you boys have been picking on each other. I am putting an end to it now!" He slammed on the brakes, pulled the car off to the side of the road, jerked his sons out and soundly spanked them both. "I don't want to hear one word out of either of you for 30 minutes!" he shouted. After a half hour of quietness, the youngest son found courage to say, "Daddy, do you remember when you spanked me? Well, one of my shoes came off . . ."

The journey into life is not without it stresses either. We are saved and sealed by the Holy Spirit, but there are days that try our sanctification. As one wit wrote:

To live above, with the saints I love

Oh, that will be glory!

To live below, with the saints I know

Well, that's a different story!

Nevertheless, we do have to live below with the saints we know. So Paul shares with us some of the ways we can make the journey less stressful.

The Law of Liberty

Romans 14:1–12

1 Receive one who is weak in the faith, but not to disputes over doubtful things.

2 For one believes he may eat all things, but he who is weak eats only vegetables.

3 Let not him who eats despise him who does not eat, and let not him who does not eat judge him who eats; for God has received him.

4 Who are you to judge another's servant? To his own master he stands or falls. Indeed, he will be made to stand, for God is able to make him stand.

5 One person esteems one day above another; another esteems every day alike. Let each be fully convinced in his own mind.

6 He who observes the day, observes it to the Lord; and he who does not observe the day, to the Lord he does not observe it. He who eats, eats to the Lord, for he gives God thanks; and he who does not eat, to the Lord he does not eat, and gives God thanks.

7 For none of us lives to himself, and no one dies to himself.

8 For if we live, we live to the Lord; and if we die, we die to the Lord. Therefore, whether we live or die, we are the Lord's.

9 For to this end Christ died and rose and lived again, that He might be Lord of both the dead and the living.

10 But why do you judge your brother? Or why do you show contempt for your brother? For we shall all stand before the judgment seat of Christ.

11 For it is written: "As I live, says the LORD, Every knee shall bow to Me, And every tongue shall confess to God."

12 So then each of us shall give account of himself to God.

Some people are control addicts. Motivated by the best of intentions, they feel they need to have the final word on every subject. They trample over other people's feelings and then wonder why everyone is upset with them. For those who have these tendencies, Paul gives some commands that will make their relationship with others less stressful:

a. *Accept legitimate differences* (vv. 1–3). Many differences exist within the body of Christ. Paul says, **For one** (the "strong" Christian) **believes he may eat all things, but he who is weak eats only vegetables**. The flesh of bulls, goats, birds and other animals was frequently offered as sacrifices before being brought to the marketplace for sale. Some Christians were so concerned about eating "meat sacrificed to idols" that they chose not to eat meat at all (1 Cor. 8:7). Others knew that "an idol is nothing in the world" (1 Cor. 8:4, cf. 1 Cor. 10:25–27) and did not worry about it. Paul wants his readers to know that both positions are fine as long as one is **fully convinced in his own mind** (v. 5). The apostle urges, however, that neither side views the other as "less spiritual." In issues that do not affect our salvation, we must allow people to follow their own conscience.

b. *Let God judge* (v. 4). Has anyone ever said to you, "So when did God die and leave you in charge?" When it comes to judging others, we sometimes act that way. There is, of course, a place in the Christian life for discernment. We are to compare outward behavior with biblical principles to see if they match. There is also a place for exhorting and even lovingly rebuking one another when behavior does not meet biblical standards. Judging, however, goes beyond this. It involves making decisions about thoughts and motives that only God truly knows. That is why God can judge but we cannot. If we try to take His place, we will find ourselves doing Satan's work. Satan is the "accuser of the brethren" (Rev. 12:10). Since God knows the hearts as well as the actions of men, it is best to let Him do the judging.

c. *Focus on the Lord* (vv. 5–8, 10–12). Instead of concentrating on the various, inconsequential differences between Christians, let's focus on the Lord. When we stand before the judgment seat of Christ, we will not have to answer for what others chose to do. We will have enough to do to explain our own choices. As Paul says, **So then each of us shall give account of himself to God** (v. 12). One day we all must look the

Lord in the eye and explain why we did (or did not do) what we did with our sacrificed lives. Therefore, make sure that you allow the Lord to work through you. If you are focused on letting the Lord live His resurrected life through your sacrificed life, what others do will be of little consequence to you.

d. *Remember Christ died for them* (v. 9). No matter how much we may disagree with our brother or sister, Christ still died for them. They may be difficult to get along with, their tongues may be sharp, and they may have a critical attitude; but Christ shed His blood at Calvary for them too. Before you write them off, remind yourself that the Father also loves them. What they are doing may grieve Him, but it does not lessen His love for them or change the fact that Christ's blood provides forgiveness for their sins as well as ours.

The Law of Love

Romans 14:13–23

13 **Therefore let us not judge one another anymore, but rather resolve this, not to put a stumbling block or a cause to fall in our brother's way.**

14 **I know and am convinced by the Lord Jesus that there is nothing unclean of itself; but to him who considers anything to be unclean, to him it is unclean.**

15 **Yet if your brother is grieved because of your food, you are no longer walking in love. Do not destroy with your food the one for whom Christ died.**

16 **Therefore do not let your good be spoken of as evil;**

17 **for the kingdom of God is not eating and drinking, but righteousness and peace and joy in the Holy Spirit.**

18 **For he who serves Christ in these things is acceptable to God and approved by men.**

19 **Therefore let us pursue the things which make for peace and the things by which one may edify another.**

20 **Do not destroy the work of God for the sake of food.**

All things indeed are pure, but it is evil for the man who eats with offense.

21 **It is good neither to eat meat nor drink wine nor do anything by which your brother stumbles or is offended or is made weak.**

22 **Do you have faith? Have it to yourself before God. Happy is he who does not condemn himself in what he approves.**

23 **But he who doubts is condemned if he eats, because he does not eat from faith; for whatever is not from faith is sin.**

In his treatise *On the Freedom of a Christian Man*, Martin Luther wrote, "A Christian man is a most free lord of all, subject to none. A Christian man is a most dutiful servant of all, subject to all." Luther highlights the dichotomy that exists in living the sacrificed life. We have marvelous freedoms. The Law, with its hundreds of rules, no longer binds us. Yet through love we are bound to consider the needs and feelings of even the least around us. Love tempers freedom. Therefore Paul says

a. *Consider other Christians first* (vv. 13, 15, 21). Paul clearly casts his lot with the strong in faith who are not given to the legalism of the weak. However, he is well aware that he may become a "stumbling block"[1] to a weaker brother whose conscience will not let him engage in the same activities as the stronger. There is no virtue in flaunting Christian liberty. Believers must not insist on their liberty in the presence of those whose conscience would be offended. To do so is not to walk in love under the lordship of Christ.

b. *Let your conscience be your guide* (vv. 14, 22–23). Christians come from many different backgrounds. Experiences from their personal lives influence what they feel comfortable doing. That is why Paul says, **to him who considers anything to be unclean, to him it is unclean** (v. 14), and, **he who doubts is condemned if he eats, because he does not eat from faith; for whatever is not from faith is sin** (v. 23). It is true that the conscience is not an infallible guide. Some people have seared

---

[1] Gk: *Proskomma* literally means an obstacle in the way, which, if one strikes his foot against, he necessarily stumbles or falls. Spiritually, it means a cause over which a soul is impelled to sin.

their conscience so they are no longer sensitive to sin. Paul's point, however, is that if a person's conscience *does* bother him, it would be a sin for him to engage in that activity no matter what someone else does.

c. *Seek peace above all* (vv. 16–17, 19). Pettiness has always plagued the church. Christians allow themselves to get sidetracked on rabbit trails while Satan monopolizes the major highways. Paul says, **for the kingdom of God is not food and drink** (v. 17). It is silly to break fellowship over peripheral issues. God is concerned about **righteousness and peace and joy in the Holy Spirit**. Squabbling about food, drink, worship days, the color of the church hymnal or the sanctuary carpet contributes neither to peace nor edification. None of this makes a person a better Christian. The basis for our fellowship is the salvation we enjoy in Christ.

It's ironic that the word *law* is qualified by the words *liberty* and *love* in the New Testament. Living the sacrificed life of Romans 12:1–2 means living in light of the law of perfect liberty we have in Christ Jesus. It also means living in light of the law of perfect love we have for the world. When what once was law in our lives is characterized by liberty and love, it no longer is law. It is life. It's what the journey into life brings to us this side of heaven.

CHAPTER 15

Burden Bearers
Romans 15:1–33

Before the invention of the automobile, most kinds of travel depended upon live burden bearers. Mules, donkeys, horses, camels and even llamas were used for this demanding task. While some of these animals were not a stylish mode of transportation, they played an essential role in conveying goods and baggage from place to place.

Since most people begin their journey into life with a lot of baggage (emotional and spiritual), Paul calls upon brothers and sisters in Christ to be burden bearers. Bearing one another's burdens may not always be fashionable or comfortable, but it is necessary.

Romans 15:1–6

1 We then who are strong ought to bear with the scruples of the weak, and not to please ourselves.

2 Let each of us please his neighbor for his good, leading to edification.

3 For even Christ did not please Himself; but as it is written, "The reproaches of those who reproached You fell on Me."

4 For whatever things were written before were written for our learning, that we through the patience and comfort of the Scriptures might have hope.

5 Now may the God of patience and comfort grant you to be like-minded toward one another, according to Christ Jesus,

6 that you may with one mind and one mouth glorify the God and Father of our Lord Jesus Christ.

An ad in the lost-and-found section of the local paper read, "LOST: Dog with three legs, blind in left eye, missing right ear and tail broken. Answers to the name of 'Lucky.'"

Some people who answer to the name of "Christian" are nearly as bad off. They struggle through life with a variety of burdens. The apostle says that brothers and sisters in Christ are to help each other carry their burdens. He specifically mentions three burdens:

a. *The burden of tolerance* (v. 1). Paul notes, **We then who are strong ought to bear with the scruples of the weak**. He is talking about the spiritually weak (cf. Rom. 14:1–3). Instead of relying on the guidance of the Holy Spirit, some Christians consult their lists of dos and don'ts. In many ways they are similar to the Pharisees, who put great stock in their interpretations and additions to the Law. Yet despite their overzealous scruples, the spiritually weak are to be welcomed as brothers and sisters in Christ. A stronger Christian should seek to avoid offending a weaker Christian even if it means refraining from activities he considers legitimate.

b. *The burden of edification* (vv. 2–3). Paul also admonishes a Christian to **please his neighbor**[1] . . . **leading to edification**. The goal is not simply to be a people pleaser but to teach those around us how a Christian responds to stresses of daily life. Many people are familiar with Henry Stanley's first words to David Livingstone ("Dr. Livingstone, I presume"), but they do not know the rest of the story. Stanley wrote some time later, "I went to Africa as prejudiced as the biggest atheist in London. But there came for me a long time for reflection. I saw this solitary old man there and asked myself, 'Why on earth does he stop here—is he cracked, or what? What is it that inspires him so?' For months after we met I found myself wondering at the old man carrying out all that was said in the Bible—'Leave all things and follow Me.' But little by little his sympathy for others became contagious; my sympathy was aroused; seeing his piety, his gentleness, his zeal, his earnestness, and how he went about his business, I was converted by him."

---

[1] Jesus' parable of The Good Samaritan defines *neighbor* in a broader sense than "the person who lives next door." Paul also uses *neighbor* to include all those who watch a Christian's behavior, whether they live across the street or across town.

Most people have not rejected true Christianity; they have never been taught what it really is. Our response to our neighbors should give them a life portrait of who Christ is and draw them to Him.

c. *The burden of unity* (vv. 5–6). Christians are admonished to be like–minded toward one another so that with **one mind and one mouth** we might **glorify the God and Father of our Lord Jesus Christ**. Disunity manifested in church splits, sour attitudes and unkind behavior brings shame to the name of Christ. Sometimes our churches seem overwhelmed by the infamous Tate family. Dick Tate tries to run everything. Ro Tate tries to change everything. Agi Tate stirs up trouble whenever possible, and Irri Tate lends him a hand. What we really need is more of this family's cousins—Facili Tate, Cogi Tate and Medi Tate.

Do not think unity means uniformity. God is not running an assembly line, turning out identical products. We are to be imitators of the Lord Jesus, not of one another (Eph. 5:1). Still, God desires and has a right to expect that His people treat one another as Christ treated them—with grace, forgiveness and love.

None of us wants to be lumped into that category that Harry Ironside described as "people who are very particular about breaking bread and very careless about breaking hearts."

On Track Again

Romans 15:7–13

7 Therefore receive one another, just as Christ also received us, to the glory of God.

8 Now I say that Jesus Christ has become a servant to the circumcision for the truth of God, to confirm the promises made to the fathers,

9 and that the Gentiles might glorify God for His mercy, as it is written: "For this reason I will confess to You among the Gentiles, And sing to Your name."

10 And again he says: "Rejoice, O Gentiles, with His people!"

11 And again: "Praise the Lᴏʀᴅ, all you Gentiles! Laud Him, all you peoples!"

12 And again, Isaiah says: "There shall be a root of Jesse; And He who shall rise to reign over the Gentiles, In Him the Gentiles shall hope."

13 Now may the God of hope fill you with all joy and peace in believing, that you may abound in hope by the power of the Holy Spirit.

A retired couple cashed in their stocks and bonds to purchase the finest motor home available. One of its best features was the cruise control. As they were traveling up the West Coast of America, the husband became tired and asked his wife to drive while he took a nap in the back. The wife obliged and immediate set the cruise control on the camper. After an hour of straight highway driving she got up to go to the bathroom. Apparently, she thought cruise control was the same as automatic pilot—at least that's what she told the highway patrol after the accident!

Israel had been on cruise control for centuries. They ignored God's plans for them to evangelize the Gentile nations. Instead, they either became involved in the pagan religions of the nations around them or they dismissed the Gentiles completely as unworthy of their evangelistic efforts. It was not until Paul was commissioned as the Apostle to the Gentiles that many of God's promises in the Old Testament to the non–Jewish peoples were taken seriously. With the Jews, the Gentiles could now

a. *Glorify God together* (v. 9). The word *glorify* means "to reveal."[2] The Gentiles and Jews were to reveal (glorify) the nature of God to those around them—especially His mercy. When people looked at the depths of depravity from which the Gentiles had been rescued, their response was one of awe. When they saw two bitter enemies like Jews and Gentiles

---

[2] In John 17:1 Jesus prays, "Father, the hour has come. Glorify Your Son, that Your Son also may glorify you." On the cross Jesus revealed both His love and the love of the Father for sinners. It was a time of revealing the heart of the Father and the Son. The word in our English language has come to mean to express awe and admiration. But this is actually a by–product. Whenever God reveals His nature (be it His love, His holiness, His righteousness, etc.), the appropriate response is to express our wonderment and reverence.

working together, they could only marvel at what the mercy of God had brought about.

b. *Rejoice together* (v. 10). The *Jewish Encyclopedia* notes that no language has as many words for *joy* and *rejoicing* as does Hebrew. In the Old Testament, 13 Hebrew roots, found in 27 words, are used primarily for some aspect of joy or joyful participation in religious worship. The Hebrew religion declares that God is the source of joy. The Gentiles could now celebrate this joy with them. Together they could rejoice in the God of their salvation.

c. *Praise together* (v. 11). The quote in verse 11 is actually a command found in Psalm 117:1. Praise is not optional for God's people; it is required. Scripture tells us that God sits "enthroned upon the praises of Israel" (Ps. 22:3, NASB). Praise is simply extolling the nature of God. It is not thanking Him for what He has done (although there is a place for that too), but it is declaring to everyone what kind of a person God is— omniscient, holy, merciful, etc. Praise is one of the ways we draw near to Him. When we stop to express what a great and wonderful God we have, His presence becomes very real to us.

Until they came to know Jesus as their Savior, the Gentiles had no understanding of God's character. The corrupt and immoral gods they worshiped could never be praised. But now, with their new knowledge of the pure and holy God, they could join their Jewish friends in praise to the One who is worthy of all praise.

d. *Hope together* (vv. 12–13). The two words we most dread to hear are *no hope*. The world has no hope. It is said that as Winston Churchill was dying he reflected on the world he had desperately tried to rescue and said, "There is no hope. There is no hope." And with that he died.

There was no hope in the Gentile world. Paul described the Ephesians as "without Christ, being aliens from the commonwealth of Israel and strangers from the covenants of promise, having no hope and without God in the world" (Eph. 2:12). But as believers in Christ, Jew and Gentile, we do have hope. The apostle continues, "But now in Christ Jesus you who once were far off have been made near by the blood of Christ" (Eph. 2:13). As a consequence of this saving hope we also have joy and peace (v. 13). Hope is the foundation for every positive and good emotion. The Holy Spirit infuses us with hope that we might be empowered to do God's will.

Lending a Helping Hand

Romans 15:14–21

14 Now I myself am confident concerning you, my brethren, that you also are full of goodness, filled with all knowledge, able also to admonish one another.

15 Nevertheless, brethren, I have written more boldly to you on some points, as reminding you, because of the grace given to me by God,

16 that I might be a minister of Jesus Christ to the Gentiles, ministering the gospel of God, that the offering of the Gentiles might be acceptable, sanctified by the Holy Spirit.

17 Therefore I have reason to glory in Christ Jesus in the things which pertain to God.

18 For I will not dare to speak of any of those things which Christ has not accomplished through me, in word and deed, to make the Gentiles obedient—

19 in mighty signs and wonders, by the power of the Spirit of God, so that from Jerusalem and round about to Illyricum I have fully preached the gospel of Christ.

20 And so I have made it my aim to preach the gospel, not where Christ was named, lest I should build on another man's foundation,

21 but as it is written: "To whom He was not announced, they shall see; And those who have not heard shall understand."

In the Old West, some men earned a living by offering their services as trail bosses. One of the primary qualifications was that they must have been over the trail before. If they had ridden the trail once successfully, then they had earned the right to do it again—and take others with them.

As you progress on your journey into life, there will be opportunities to help others to cover that part of the trail you have been over. Your experience will be an invaluable asset to those not as far along on the journey as you. The apostle Paul reveals some personal traits that will help you be the kind of a spiritual guide God wants you to be:

a. *Tactfulness* (v. 14). Paul took great care to assure the Christians at Rome that he had confidence in them. He did not nag them. He was simply reminding them of something they already knew. He knew that tact was lacking in Christian circles then—as it is today. He also knew that a tactful approach would produce more fruit than an insensitive one. Leading others along the journey into life is more fruitful when we are tactful.

b. *Graciousness* (vv. 15–16). A woman was out shopping one day and bought a bag of cookies. Having put them in her purse, she decided to stop at the coffee shop for a cup of coffee. All the tables were filled except for one at which a man sat reading a newspaper. Seating herself in the opposite chair, she opened her purse, took out a magazine and began reading. After a while, she reached for a cookie, only to see the man across from her also taking a cookie. She glared at him; he just smiled at her. Moments later she reached for another cookie, just as the man also took one. Angry, she stared at the one remaining cookie—whereupon the man reached over, broke the cookie in half and offered her a piece. She grabbed it and stuffed it into her mouth as the man smiled and left. The woman was steaming as she opened her purse to put her magazine away. There she saw her bag of cookies. She had been helping herself to the cookies belonging to the gracious man whose table she had shared!

The grace showed by that man is the kind of grace God shows to us—undeserved and sometimes ungratefully received. This is also the kind of grace we need to share with those whom God gives us to nurture in the faith.

c. *Humility* (vv. 17–18). Paul never allowed his successes to become a source of pride. Instead he says, **For I will not dare to speak of any of those things which Christ has not accomplished through me.** Where we are on our spiritual journey is not the result of human efforts but of God working in and through us. Humility allows us to share with others without condemning them. We know that at one time we were just like them, and except for the grace of God, we would be just like them still.

d. *Reliance on divine power* (v. 19). Jonathan Edwards was a brilliant theologian whose sermons had an overwhelming impact on those who heard him. One in particular, his famous "Sinners in the Hands of an Angry God," moved hundreds of people to repentance and salvation. That single message helped spark the revival known as The Great Awakening (1734–1744).

From a human standpoint, it seems incredible that such far-reaching results could come from one message. Edwards did not have a commanding voice or impressive pulpit manner. He used few gestures, and he read from a manuscript. Yet God's Spirit moved upon his hearers with conviction and power.

Unless we minister in the power of the Spirit, all we do is in vain. Paul does not credit the success of his ministry to his own efforts but **by the power of the Spirit of God**. As we seek to help others, let us learn to lean on God's Spirit and not our own wisdom.

e. *Courageousness* (vv. 20–21). The apostle did not choose the easiest path. Paul was not interested in places where the foundation had already been laid. By the time he wrote this letter to the Romans, he was likely in his early fifties. Still, like Caleb, who at age 85 asked for the most difficult part of Caanan to conquer (Josh. 14:10), Paul was not ready to coast. He sought territory where people had not heard the Gospel.

It takes courage to minister to others, to get involved in people's lives. In his book *The Yoke of Christ*, Elton Trueblood quotes a letter from a schoolgirl who probes the depth of her soul. She writes, "I've been thinking much this year about the importance of caring, of the passion of life. I've often realized that it takes courage to care. Caring is dangerous. It leaves you open to hurt and to looking like a fool. And perhaps it's because they have been hurt so often that people are afraid to care. You can't die if you're not alive. I have found many places in my own life where I keep a secret store of indifference as a sort of self-protection."

This young girl shows penetrating insight. We must have the courage to care, because Christ cared, even though it meant a cross.

A Special Place

Romans 15:22–29

22 For this reason I also have been much hindered from coming to you.

23 But now no longer having a place in these parts, and having a great desire these many years to come to you,

24 whenever I journey to Spain, I shall come to you. For I hope to see you on my journey, and to be helped on my way there by you, if first I may enjoy your company for a while.

25 But now I am going to Jerusalem to minister to the saints.

26 For it pleased those from Macedonia and Achaia to make a certain contribution for the poor among the saints who are in Jerusalem.

27 It pleased them indeed, and they are their debtors. For if the Gentiles have been partakers of their spiritual things, their duty is also to minister to them in material things.

28 Therefore, when I have performed this and have sealed to them this fruit, I shall go by way of you to Spain.

29 But I know that when I come to you, I shall come in the fullness of the blessing of the gospel of Christ.

As we travel, each place we visit has its own special attraction. There is the peacefulness of a Minnesota lake, the majesty of the Swiss Alps, the awesomeness of the ocean waves. While we may have our personal favorites, together they make up the fabric of our journey.

As Paul shares his travel plans, each destination has its own special attraction. Together, they cover some of the important aspects of a spiritual journey:

a. *Rome: to fellowship with the saints* (v. 24). Paul is not ashamed to admit to the Roman believers that he looked forward to the time when he would be able to **enjoy [their] company for a while**. Fellowship is an important part of our spiritual journey. Someone has compared the

Christian life to a coal from a fireplace. Left among the other coals it burns brightly; placed alone on the hearth it cools and dies.

When the poet Goethe was drawing his last breath he cried, "Light, light, the world needs more light." Years later another poet wrote, "Goethe was wrong; what he should have said was, 'Warmth, warmth, the world needs more warmth.' We shall not die from the darkness but from the cold." Actually, both are important. The Gospel gives us light; fellowship gives us warmth. The opportunity to enjoy the warmth of Christian fellowship is a special attraction on our journey.

b. *Jerusalem: to minister to the needy* (vv. 25–27). The Jewish Christians were experiencing difficult times. Since occupations in Jerusalem were strongly related to the temple and temple practices, Jews who became Christians usually were out of a job. Some could no longer, in good conscience, be a part of the temple system. Others who did not voluntarily leave were thrown out by the priests as soon as they discovered the workers' faith in Christ. This left many families impoverished. Paul had a strong desire to bring a gift from the Gentile Christians to relieve the poverty of Jerusalem's Christians.

Suffering is common in our world. Jesus frequently encountered it in His sojourn on earth. Ten times the Scriptures say that Jesus looked on the crowds or individuals and had compassion upon them. This is one of the marks of a true Christian.

Tradition tells us that Justin, one of the early church fathers, was going home one cold evening when he came upon a beggar sitting along the road. Justin had no money—in fact, nothing except a tattered, old army cloak. Feeling compassion for the beggar, he took his cloak, cut it in half, gave half to the beggar and wrapped himself in the other half.

That night he dreamed he saw Jesus walking about heaven wrapped in half of an old army cloak. One of the angels asked, "Jesus, why are you wearing that old, tattered piece of cloak?" Jesus looked at him, smiled gently and said, "Because my friend Justin gave it to me."

The Christian whose heart cannot bleed when other hearts are bleeding needs to question his salvation.

c. *Spain: to share the gospel with the lost* (v. 28). Of all the parts of the Christian life—fellowship, service and evangelism—the latter had the greatest hold on Paul's heart. He never got used to the sound of millions of feet on the path to hell.

Often Christians settle for being the keepers of the stained glass aquarium instead of fishers of men. We have programs and conferences, seminars and videos, but we never get around to evangelizing the lost. Paul wouldn't tolerate this.

A newly hired salesman sent in his first written report. It was evident that he was nearly illiterate. He wrote: "I seen this outfit who ain't never bought a dimes worth of nothin from us and sole them some goods. I am now going to Chicawgo." But before he could be fired, a second letter arrived. It read: "I came to Chicawgo an sole them haff a millyon." Hesitant to dismiss the man, yet afraid of what would happen if he didn't, the sales manager dumped the problem into the president's lap. The next day the staff was amazed to see those two reports on the bulletin board, with this memo from the president: "We ben spendin two much time trying to spel insted of tryin to sel. I want everbody should read these letters fom Gooch, who is doin a grate job, and you should go out and DO LIKE HE DONE!"

Of course the president was not extolling the virtues of incorrect spelling or improper grammar. But his point was clear, as Paul's point should be clear to us. We must stop spending all our time learning how to evangelize and just do it. Nothing succeeds like success, and success comes only by practice, not by theory.

Prayer Support

Romans 15:30–33

30 Now I beg you, brethren, through the Lord Jesus Christ, and through the love of the Spirit, that you strive together with me in prayers to God for me,

31 that I may be delivered from those in Judea who do not believe, and that my service for Jerusalem may be acceptable to the saints,

32 that I may come to you with joy by the will of God, and may be refreshed together with you.

169

33 Now the God of peace be with you all. Amen.

Every traveler needs support personnel, from auto clubs to towing services. These agencies supply directions, travel tips, emergency assistance and anything else needed to get the traveler to his destination. Such travel services sometimes make the difference between a smooth, successful journey and an arduous one.

As spiritual travelers we, too, need support personnel—especially those who will support us in prayer. Paul specifies three areas of significant prayer concern:

a. *Safety from those who don't believe* (v. 31). In Paul's day this danger was always present. He tells the Corinthian Christians, "Three times I was beaten with rods; once I was stoned; three times I was shipwrecked; a night and a day I have been in the deep; in journeys often, in perils of waters, in perils of robbers, in perils of my own countrymen, in perils of the Gentiles, in perils in the city, in perils in the wilderness, in perils in the sea, in perils among false brethren" (2 Cor. 11:25–26). Given the realities of travel in the Roman Empire, it's no surprise that Paul asks for deliverance.

There is still danger today. Two missionaries from New Tribes Mission, Tim Van Dyke and Steve Welsh, were kidnapped in January 1994 by rebel soldiers in Columbia. In June 1995 they were killed in a skirmish between their captors and soldiers from the Columbian army. Many others over the decades have met a similar fate. A significant ministry we all can have is to pray for our brothers and sisters who serve in dangerous places.

b. *Acceptance from those who do believe* (v. 31). But not all the danger comes from unbelievers. Some who claim to be Christians still spurn the teaching of the Word. The apostle John wrote of a man named Diotrephes, "who loves to have the preeminence" and who "does not receive us" (3 John 1:9). The church still has its share of men and women like Diotrephes who want to control and refuse correction even when it is from the Word. Let's pray like the little girl who asked God to "please make all the bad people good, and the good people nice."

c. *That God's will be done* (v. 32). Paul wanted to come to them, but he wanted to do so **by the will of God**. We may be confident of what His will is, but we still need to let God take care of the details. It may come about in a way we never considered. Paul certainly did not expect to be delivered to the Romans as a political prisoner, but that was God's will. As we pray, let's remember to pray that God's will be done in His way and in His time.

CHAPTER 16

Journey Mates
Romans 16:1–27

What is a journey without friends? We have arrived at the final chapter of Romans, and Paul makes it clear that on his journey into life he had made numerous friends. When you consider that the apostle had never been to the church at Rome, he greets an extraordinary number of people. Some scholars point to this as an indication Paul did not write the last chapter. A better explanation is that he had met many of these people (such as Aquila and Priscilla) elsewhere during his wide–ranging travels. Others he knew through extended family and friendship ties. *Networking* may be a computer–age word, but the practice was thriving in the first century. One thing is clear: Paul had a heart for people—and so should we. Friends make the journey much more fun.

The Dependable Friend

Romans 16:1–2

1 I commend to you Phoebe our sister, who is a servant of the church in Cenchrea,

2 that you may receive her in the Lord in a manner worthy of the saints, and assist her in whatever business she has need of you; for indeed she has been a helper of many and of myself also.

In the Walker Art Gallery in Liverpool, England, hangs Poynter's magnificent picture, "Faithful Unto Death." The painting depicts a Roman guard on duty while the palace behind him is destroyed by the eruption of Mount Vesuvius. The dead lay all around him, while others flee for their lives. Yet the stoic guard stands like a marble statue, faithfully staying at his post even though it meant his death.

How rarely we find such dependability. Yet Phoebe, Paul's friend, was that kind of person. She was so dependable that Paul entrusted into her care the most important letter he ever wrote. Phoebe demonstrates some of the characteristics that are important to dependability:

a. *A servant's heart* (v.1). Paul tells the Christians at Rome, **I commend to you Phoebe our sister, who is a servant**[1] **of the church in Cenchrea.**[2] The word used for *servant* in this verse means "one who executes the commands of another." It was frequently used to refer to household servants, people who did only what they were told. A visitor at a leprosy hospital watched as a nurse tenderly cared for the ulcerated sores of a leper. With a shudder, the visitor said, "I wouldn't do that for a million dollars!" "Neither would I," the nurse replied, "but I do it for Jesus for nothing." We serve others not for personal gain but because the Lord commanded us to.

b. *A courageous heart* (v. 2). The Christians at Rome are admonished to **receive her in the Lord in a manner worthy of the saints, and assist her in whatever business she has need of you.** Evidently, Phoebe had no friends or family in Rome. It took a tremendous amount of courage to undertake a trip of this magnitude, considering the dangers and rigors of travel in those days and the unknown elements of a strange city. No one would have thought the worse had Phoebe decided to back out—but she was dependable. In the face of danger, hardship and uncertainty, she had the courage to do what needed to be done.

c. *A generous heart* (v. 2). The fact that Phoebe was able to make such a trip indicated she was a woman of means. But she was also a woman who shared what God had given her. Paul says, **For indeed she has been a helper**[3] **of many and of myself also.** Friends who freely give of themselves in addition to their wealth are truly exercising their dependability.

---

[1] Gk: *diakonos* is also translated "deacon." Hence, some translate this "deaconess." It can represent either the office (deacon) or the general idea of service.

[2] Cenchrea served as the seaport for Corinth toward the east on the Saronic Gulf.

[3] Gk: *prostatis* literally means "one who stands by in case of need." It was used in classical Greek to describe a trainer in the Olympic Games, who stood by the athletes to see that they were properly trained.

Ministry Friends

Romans 16:3–16

3 Greet Priscilla and Aquila, my fellow workers in Christ Jesus,

4 who risked their own necks for my life, to whom not only I give thanks, but also all the churches of the Gentiles.

5 Likewise greet the church that is in their house. Greet my beloved Epaenetus, who is the firstfruits of Achaia to Christ.

6 Greet Mary, who labored much for us.

7 Greet Andronicus and Junia, my kinsmen and my fellow prisoners, who are of note among the apostles, who also were in Christ before me.

8 Greet Amplias, my beloved in the Lord.

9 Greet Urbanus, our fellow worker in Christ, and Stachys, my beloved.

10 Greet Apelles, approved in Christ. Greet those who are of the household of Aristobulus.

11 Greet Herodion, my kinsman. Greet those who are of the household of Narcissus who are in the Lord.

12 Greet Tryphena and Tryphosa, who have labored in the Lord. Greet the beloved Persis, who labored much in the Lord.

13 Greet Rufus, chosen in the Lord, and his mother and mine.

14 Greet Asyncritus, Phlegon, Hermas, Patrobas, Hermes, and the brethren who are with them.

15 Greet Philologus and Julia, Nereus and his sister, and Olympas, and all the saints who are with them.

16 Greet one another with a holy kiss. The churches of Christ greet you.

A study done by researchers at Ohio State University Medical School revealed that fellowship with friends can actually improve our health by protecting the body's immune system. In our stress–filled society, we can use the healing touch of friendship as much as a dose of vitamins. The apostle Paul may not have known about immunology, but he instinctively knew that friends were good for him, so he made lots of them. In this portion of Scripture he greets 24 people by name, in addition to five households. Paul's approach to friendship demonstrates some principles that we can use as well:

a. *Make your friendships intimate.* Paul ministered to thousands of people, yet he knew every friend by name. For seven years John Fawcett had ministered at a small Baptist church in Wainsgate, England. Then he got a call to serve the large, prestigious Carter Lane Church in London. Fawcett accepted and loaded his possessions on the wagon, but that was as far as he got. The friendships were too deep; the relationships were too intimate for him to leave. He unloaded the wagon and stayed for another 54 years. Out of this experience came the hymn *Blest Be the Tie That Binds.*

In many churches there is no intimacy. We are identified by the numbers on our offering envelopes and consider ourselves fortunate if the pastor recognizes our face. Even the worship hour can be impersonal as we sit next to strangers week after week. How many of us could name 24 friends in our church? God meant for friendships to be on an intimate basis.

b. *Make your friendships broad.* When you read through this list of names, you find people with Jewish names, like **Priscilla and Aquila,** and those with Greek names, such as **Hermas** and **Olympas.** There are relatively new Christians, like **Epaenetus, who is the firstfruits of Achaia,** and more mature Christians, such as **Andronicus and Junia, . . . who also were in Christ before me.** There were both men and women, which is unusual because rabbis, which Paul once was, were forbidden to have contact with women. It's evident that Paul had quite an assortment of friends.

Sometimes we make the mistake of establishing relationships only with people of like mind. Yet carbon copy Christians are seldom beneficial to one another. There is real benefit to fellowshipping with Christians who differ from us in their theology (as long as we agree on the essentials), and there is a need to have friendships with non–Christians. Salt does no good if it stays in the salt shaker. So make friendships that are both broad and deep.

c. *Make your friendships real.* Imitations are readily available today. We have fake jewelry, fake leather, even fake food. Imitation may be the sincerest form of flattery, but it's a poor basis for friendship. Paul says, **Greet one another with a holy kiss.** Though this is not a common practice in Western culture, a hug, a warm handshake or a slap on the back are ways we say, "I care about you." Don't wait until your friends are gone to say in a tangible way, "I love you. You're special to me." Be a real friend; fake friendships never stand the test of time.

Difficult Friendships

Romans 16:17–20

17 Now I urge you, brethren, note those who cause divisions and offenses, contrary to the doctrine which you learned, and avoid them.

18 For those who are such do not serve our Lord Jesus Christ, but their own belly, and by smooth words and flattering speech deceive the hearts of the simple.

19 For your obedience has become known to all. Therefore I am glad on your behalf; but I want you to be wise in what is good, and simple concerning evil.

20 And the God of peace will crush Satan under your feet shortly. The grace of our Lord Jesus Christ be with you. Amen.

God seems to give us one or more friends who challenge our sanctification. It may be an ungodly coworker or a family member who claims Christ as Savior but whose life doesn't show it. Paul indicates that how you treat them depends on their problem.

a. *If they are in blatant doctrinal error, avoid them* (vv. 17–18). Verse 17 says, **Now I urge you, brethren, note those who cause divisions and offenses, contrary to the doctrine which you learned, and avoid them.** Paul has both actions and attitudes in mind. By their actions (accompanied by their false teaching) they were causing divisions within the church. By their attitudes they were causing offenses in the church. God intends the church to be a place of unity and acceptance. If any person will not conform to His intent, he is to be shunned. This serves a twofold purpose. It isolates the error and keeps it from spreading. Furthermore, it reinforces the seriousness of the sin and hopefully will lead the person to repentance and restoration.

b. *If they are in blind ignorance, teach them* (v. 19). In the latter part of verse 19, Paul admonishes us to **be wise in what is good, and simple concerning evil.** When John A. Broadus was the president of Southern Baptist Theological Seminary in Louisville, Kentucky, he went to a country church to preach one Sunday. A man approached him after the service and said, "Brother, God kin git along without all your learnin'." Broadus replied, "Yes, sir, God can. And He can also get along without your ignorance." A seminary degree is not required to understand the Bible, but spiritual ignorance can be disastrous. H. Grotius suggests that Christians ought to be "too good to deceive, too wise to be deceived."

Yet we must genuinely reach out to those who are in the clutches of honest ignorance. Aquila and Priscilla demonstrated that with Apollos (Acts 18:26). James commends it in James 5:19–20, "Brethren, if anyone among you wanders from the truth, and someone turns him back, let him know that he who turns a sinner from the error of his way will save a soul from death and cover a multitude of sins." We are to know the truth and make it known as well.

c. *If they are in bondage to sin, deliver them* (v. 20). We are always to hate the sinner's sin, but we also must realize the real source of the problem is Satan. We have the promise, however, that **the God of peace will crush Satan under your feet shortly.** Remember, our battle is not against flesh and blood but against principalities and powers of darkness (Eph. 6:12). When we direct our warfare toward the root cause, Satan, he will be defeated and souls will be delivered.

Honored Friends

Romans 16:21–24

21 Timothy, my fellow worker, and Lucius, Jason, and Sosipater, my kinsmen, greet you.

22 I, Tertius, who wrote this epistle, greet you in the Lord.

23 **Gaius, my host and the host of the whole church, greets you. Erastus, the treasurer of the city, greets you, and Quartus, a brother.**

24 **The grace of our Lord Jesus Christ be with you all. Amen.**

Not all friends are created equal. Nor do they need to be. In the midst of many friends, some friends bear special mention. Elisha had his "sons of the prophets" (2 Kings 4:38 ff). Of the multitudes that followed Him, Jesus had His twelve. Paul also had special friends. Special friends can fall into several categories:

a. *Servant friends* (vv. 21-22). These are the friends who serve God with us. Timothy was one of Paul's converts from Lystra and became a travel colleague with him. The apostle had a special spot in his heart for this young man and told the Philippians, "For I have no one like-minded, who will sincerely care for your state. . . . But you know his proven character, that as a son with his father he served with me in the gospel" (Phil. 2:20, 22). Tertius, the one who wrote this letter as Paul dictated it, was another friend who was bound to Paul through service. Nothing binds our hearts together as much as serving alongside one another.

b. *Family friends* (vv. 21-23). Lucius, Jason and Sosipater are called **my kinsmen**. This would indicate that they were probably Jewish Christians. Quartus is designated as **brother** and was likely a Gentile. As believers in Christ, however, Jews and Gentiles are both part of God's family and share common family ties. If our friends are Christians, they are family. Having friends who are brothers and sisters in Christ is a tremendous privilege. These are truly "forever friends" because we will have a relationship with them throughout eternity.

c. *Gracious friends* (v. 23). Gaius and Erastus were both known for their gracious generosity. Gaius[4] was **the host of the whole church**, but he was probably also the one who provided housing for Paul at Corinth, according to Acts 18:7. Erastus is noted in this passage as **the treasurer**

---

[4] The Roman system of naming a citizen was by the use of three names (*praenomen, nomen and cognomen*). Gaius was a common *praenomen*. His full name would have been Gaius Titus Justus.

of the city. In 1929, in the city of Corinth, Greece, a Latin inscription was found engraved on a marble paving block. It read, "Erastus, commissioner for public works, laid this pavement at his own expense." The pavement dates back to the first century and may have been the work of Paul's gracious friend. Friends who have open homes and open hearts are as precious as they are rare.

What kind of a friend are you?

Journey's End

Romans 16:25–27

25 Now to Him who is able to establish you according to my gospel and the preaching of Jesus Christ, according to the revelation of the mystery which was kept secret since the world began

26 but now has been made manifest, and by the prophetic Scriptures has been made known to all nations, according to the commandment of the everlasting God, for obedience to the faith—

27 to God, alone wise, be glory through Jesus Christ forever. Amen.

Every journey, no matter how tranquil or turbulent, has to come to an end. That it is a journey implies a destination. In fact, the destination is crucial because it determines whether the journey has been worthwhile.

Paul thus draws his journey to a close. We had the point of departure (all have sinned), the method of travel (salvation through faith alone) and scenic high points along the way. Now he comes to our destination—the presence of God our Father. As we experience the marvel of an intimate relationship with God, Paul implies that we will have the privilege of knowing:

a. *The all–powerful God* (v. 25). God is powerful enough **to establish you**. The word *establish* means to "fix firmly." We need not fear that the trials of our journey will move us. A little girl listened attentively as her father lead the family devotions. She seemed awed by her parents' talk of

God's limitless power and mercy. "Daddy," she asked, placing her little hands on his knees, "how big is God?" Her father thought for a moment and answered, "Honey, He is always just a little bigger than you need."

b. *The everlasting God* (v. 26). Eternity is beyond our comprehension, but God encompasses it all. The psalmist says, "Even from everlasting to everlasting, You are God" (Ps. 90:2). Contemplating our eternal God is a sure cure for any feelings of self–importance or grandeur. Yet it overwhelms us that an infinite God could have such love and commitment for finite creatures like us.

c. *The all–wise God* (v. 27). Much that passes for human wisdom is sheer foolishness. In 1990 scientists discovered what they thought was a 16-million–year–old fossilized dinosaur egg. Later they determined it was a stomach stone from a cow who threw it up just five years earlier. Their explanation: "Mother Nature fooled us." It is comforting to know that God can never be fooled and His wisdom is always available to us. James says, "If any of you lacks wisdom, let him ask of God, who gives to all liberally and without reproach, and it will be given to him" (James 1:5).

How Far
Have You Come?

A little boy was offered the opportunity to select a dog for his birthday present. At the pet store he was shown a number of puppies. From them he picked one whose tail was wagging furiously. When he was asked why he selected that particular dog, the little boy said, "I wanted the one with the happy ending."

When we begin our journey into life, we are assured of a happy ending. Paul says in Philippians 1:6, "Being confident of this very thing, that He who has begun a good work in you will complete it until the day of Jesus Christ." God will never back out of the promises He makes to those who receive Christ as their Savior.

But our journey begins in a rather hopeless and discouraging condition. Whether we are Jews or Gentiles, whether we follow a divinely revealed law or make up one of our own, we inevitably fail. We fall short. We have no peace. We are burdened with guilt and shame, with no way to help ourselves.

Then comes the good news. Paul says, "While we were still sinners, Christ died for us" (Rom. 5:8). All of man's attempts to reach God have failed. Many times our attempts follow admirable principles: Do not kill. Do not cheat. Live in peace with one another. But no law presents a solution for those times when we transgress it. Only God, reaching down to man through Jesus Christ, has provided the solvent for the stain of sin. Scripture says that God has reconciled us to Himself through Jesus Christ (2 Cor. 5:18). When we accept Him as our Savior, we begin the journey into life.

Have you begun that journey? Do you know the Lord? I mean *really* know the Lord? Some people know the Lord the way they know, say, Winston Churchill—they know *about* Him. They know that Jesus lived and can recall some of the things He did.

Some people knew Jesus this way in His day too. When Jesus encountered a demon-possessed man at the Capernaum synagogue, the demon said, "What have we to do with You, Jesus of Nazareth? Did You come to destroy us? I know who You, who You are—the Holy One of God!" (Luke 4:34). The demon not only knew Jesus' name, but he also knew Jesus was the Holy One of God.

Nicodemus, the ruler of the Jews who came to Jesus at night, knew He was "a teacher come from God; for no one can do these signs that You do unless God is with him" (John 3:2). He knew of Jesus' fame as a miracle worker, but he would soon come to know Him in a far different way. If you read the words of Jesus to Nicodemus in this passage, a whole new way of knowing the Lord opens up to you. Nicodemus placed his faith in Jesus as Savior and really knew Him for the first time. He was born again.

It is not enough to know *about* Jesus. Even the demons admit that much (James 2:19). Those who simply know the Lord on this level are condemned because of their sins and need to trust Christ as Savior.

When the Samaritan woman left the well and told everyone about Jesus, they came from the city to see Him. While not everyone believed her story, many said, "Now we believe, not because of what you said, for we have heard for ourselves and we know that this is indeed the Christ, the Savior of the world" (John 4:42). These Samaritans moved from only knowing about Jesus to a saving faith in Him.

The disciples moved to that level as well. But they also learned that there is more to knowing the Lord than trusting Him as Savior. In John 14 Jesus said to them, "If you had known Me, you would have known My Father also; and from now on you know Him and have seen Him" (v. 7). It is evident from Peter's confession (Matt. 16:16) that the disciples trusted Him as their Savior. Two verses later He asked, "Have I been with you so long, and yet you have not known Me, Philip?" (v. 9). Of course

Philip knew the Lord. He was a believer. He knew Jesus personally as Savior and Lord. So what did Jesus mean by this question? Philip and the other disciples knew Jesus, but it is evident that much more intimacy was possible in their relationship with Him.

The apostle Paul longed for that kind of intimacy as well. He wrote from his prison in Rome of his desire to "know Him and the power of His resurrection, and the fellowship of His sufferings" (Phil. 3:10). He wanted to rise above the entry level of faith to the intimacy of hungering and thirsting after righteousness (Matt. 5:6). He wanted to know the Lord on the highest and deepest level possible. Paul did not seek some mystical knowledge of the Lord or a hidden secret about Him. Neither did he seek a deeper experience that could be enjoyed only by a few. Paul simply wanted to know the Lord in a more intimate and worshipful way than he did.

The Choice Is Yours

The journey into life is long. It lasts a life time. But no journey comes to an end unless we take the first steps to begin it. Have you started your journey into life? Have you asked Jesus to be your Savior and to forgive you for your sins? If not, you can right now, right where you are. Just pray to God and admit that you are a sinner and need a Savior. Tell Him you believe only Jesus paid the price to be your Savior, and then ask Jesus Christ to come into your life and save you. He will, if you ask Him.

The Bible says, "But as many as received Him, to them He gave the right to become children of God, to those who believe in His name" (John 1:12). The apostle John also says,

> And this is the testimony: that God has given us eternal life, and this life is in His Son. He who has the Son has life; he who does not have the Son of God does not have life. These things I have written to you who believe in the name of the Son of God, that you may know that you have eternal life, and that you may continue to believe in the name of the Son of God (1 John 5:11-13).

Journey Into Life

If you have started the journey into life, how far are you along the way? The late Vance Havner used to say, "How long you've been a Christian only tells how long you've been on the road; it doesn't tell how far you've come." Take positive steps to get to know the Lord more intimately and worshipfully today. Spend time with Him in prayer and in the meaningful study of His Word. Make sure your life is clean and pleasing to Him.

The journey into life is the most exciting and interesting journey you will ever take. Don't be content to be an armchair traveler. Pack up your bags and get started today!

A Selected Bibliography

Finegan, Jack. *Light From the Ancient Past.* Princeton: Princeton University Press, 1946.

Ramsay, Sir William. *St. Paul the Traveller and the Roman Citizen.* Grand Rapids: Baker Book House, 1949.

Miller, Adam W. *An Introduction to the New Testament.*

Lewis, C. S. *Mere Christianity.* New York: The Macmillan Company, 1952.

Packer, James I. *Fundamentalism and the Word of God.*

Godet, Fredrich. *Commentary on Romans.* Grand Rapids: Kregel Publishers, 1977.

Trench, R. C. *Synonyms of the New Testament.* Marshallton, Delaware: The National Foundation for Christian Education.

Vine, W. E. *Expository Dictionary of Old and New Testament Words.* Old Tappan, New Jersey: Fleming H. Revell Company, 1981.

Morris, Leon. *The Epistle to the Romans.* Grand Rapids, Michigan: William B. Eerdmans Publishing Company, 1988.

Barclay, William. *The Letter to the Romans.* Philadelphia: The Westminster Press, 1975.

Barna, George. *The Barna Report.* Ventura, California: Gospel Light's Regal Books, 1992-93.

Richardson, Alan. *A Theological Word Book of the Bible.* New York: The Macmillan Company, 1971.

Dunn, Ronald. *Don't Just Stand There—Pray Something.* San Bernardino, California: Here's Life Publishers, Inc., 1991.

Kroll, Woodrow M. *Liberty Bible Commentary on the New Testament.* Nashville, Tennessee: Thomas Nelson Inc., Publishers, 1978.

Back to the Bible is a nonprofit ministry dedicated to Bible teaching, evangelism and edification of Christians worldwide.

If we may assist you in knowing more about Christ and the Christian life, please write to us without obligation.

Back to the Bible
P.O. Box 82808
Lincoln, NE 68501